RELIGIOUS SPIRITS

The Blight IN *the Churches*

Peter Hobson

This book is an expanded extract of chapter 3 from a major publication entitled **"We ALL Have Our Demons"**. The major book also carries chapters dealing with -

> Superstition, Multiple Personality Disorder (and D.I.D.), Profanity, Stupidity, Fears, Sickness, Cancer, Death, False Memory Syndrome, Schizophrenia, Bitterness, Anger, Epilepsy, Reincarnation, Blasphemy, the Man of Sin, The Occult – and more! (see last page)

We hope you can obtain a copy.

1st Edition 2004

Bible translations are from various sources, and are sometimes my own translation.

National Library of Australia
I.S.B.N. 0 947252 12 6

Printed in Sri Lanka
by New Life Literature (Pvt) Ltd.
Katunayake, SRI LANKA

CONTENTS

RELIGIOUS SPIRITS
The Blight IN The Churches

INTRODUCTION

The Mixture - The Search

FOREWORD

Religious Spirits will not be a popular book with "religious" people. It does, however, state important spiritual truths for those who are spiritually mature and ready to receive strong meat.

As an example, Peter's statement that *"it is so easy for a stage presentation to degenerate into entertainment for the audience on earth, rather than worship for the Audience on the Throne in Heaven,"* is so very true that it will prick wayward flesh. But Jesus did say He was come to bring a sword – a sword which is the Word of God – so powerful and sharp that it would *pierce even to the dividing asunder of soul and spirit, and of the joints and marrow, and is a discerner of the thoughts and intents of the heart.*

It is extremely important in this hour that we each search our own hearts, purify our motives before the Lord, and fully yield to Him in order to be faithful and ready servants when He appears...and so that we may help others who are lost and perishing in this fallen world.

Bill Banks, President
Impact Christian Books Inc.
Kirkwood, Missouri
USA

PREFACE

I just can't believe what has happened! This book began as a lift-out booklet from chapter 3 of our major publication **"We ALL Have Our Demons"**.

Then the Lord began to add to it – and add to it – and add to it.

I couldn't stop writing! How many times I thought this text was completed and requested our faithful missionary printers, New Life Literature in Katunayake, Sri Lanka, to finally typeset the text, only to apologise as more material came flooding onto my desk and into my brain.

I hope you find it as Holy Spirit inspired as anything else you have read written by a "modern" author.

RELIGIOUS SPIRITS

INTRODUCTION

> *"I could scarcely reconcile myself at first to this strange way of preaching in the fields, of which he (Whitefield) set me an example on Sunday; I had been all my life (till very lately) so tenacious of every point relating to decency and order that I should have thought the saving of souls almost a sin if it had not been done in a church".*
> *John Wesley 29 March 1739*

– confessing his RELIGIOUS churchianity. No wonder the good Lord forced him into the open air to preach!

When I read this entry in Wesley's Journal it reminded me very much of my astonishment when as a young man (teenager?) I read that **Pat Boone,** the sales record-breaking recording artist and film star, had baptized someone in a Hollywood swimming pool (the ultimate luxury symbol at that time).

How could he do that, I wondered? Don't baptisms have to be carried out by an ordained minister and in a church (building)? Such were the religious, cultural limitations imposed on many of us at that time.

Have you ever been on holidays and wondered where you would go to worship when Sunday came around? For **Orthodox** and **Roman Catholic** Christians, this usually poses little problem, but for **Protestants** who are aware of the main themes of the Bible's teaching, especially Christians into

Renewal (Charismatics), it can be a major head-ache. From the **Anglo-Catholic (Anglican)** tradition to **Toronto**-style experiences it's so hard to find a church today to "suit" an informed, born-again, Bible-believing worshipper who wants to worship "in spirit/Spirit and in truth" (John 4:24).

The Mixture

If you are not careful you could find yourself surrounded by idols (graven images) and crucifixes, ministers who call themselves "priests" and dress in glorious apparel, right down to the "beat" generation who put on a rock concert with its noise and drum beat hypnosis. It seems to me that whenever I go to other churches to meet with the Lord I have to suffer something unclean as well, as part of the "package".

Through most church assemblies there runs a stream of the truth of God's Word but often it is surrounded by so much spiritual pollution I personally can't always face it and prefer to stay home for private devotions - and then I feel guilty (Heb. 10:25).

I wonder how many Christians out there in "Western" nations instinctively feel the same way, perhaps without being able to put it into words?

I'm all for people going to church but simply going and learning to do religious forms physically (kneeling etc.) WITHOUT meeting with Jesus personally and spiritually, tends to make us ritualistic, and therefore "religious". Also **religious spirits** tend to belong to a grouping which includes **legalistic, critical, condemnatory** and **accusing spirits**. They can be mixed up with a lot of Holy Spirit too (hence the two-souled[1] Christian), so sometimes it is very difficult

1   "Two-souled", usually translated "double-minded" - James 1:8, 4:8.

to discern the mixture that comes out of our mouths (James 3:8-10). One has only to think of the mixture that sometimes comes forth from the mouth of a modern prophet in the assembly. If it is any consolation the Apostle Paul testifies to his old religiosity (e.g. Acts 22:3-5) before he met with Jesus, was broken in spirit by physical blindness, and set free to SEE, physically AND spiritually, by the fullness of the Spirit of God (Acts 9:1-9).

The Search

How can you tell if you have a religious spirit? Well, the truth is most people have - especially if they have been TAUGHT religious practices and habits as a little child.

We are all born with a significant religious need and capacity which forces mankind to inquire, to search for truth and answers to questions regarding the meaning of life. Why were we born? Why do we die? What "gods" can help me? What are the "laws" of life, the universe (creation) etc. ???

The Lord has created this spiritual area within us, *the Holy of Holies in each human temple/house created by Him and for Him to dwell within,* and even if we let the **Man of Sin[2]** enter where he ought not (2 Thess. 2:3-4) he can only partially "satisfy" our religious needs.

---

2   The application of this personality dwelling in a human being rather than in a Temple built in Jerusalem is discussed in Chapter 7 **"We ALL Have Our Demons"**.

CHAPTER 1

RELIGION AND CHRISTIANITY

I am sure many of you readers have heard people say **"I'm sick of religion"**, especially if you have a ministry of personal evangelism which you seek to use in the market place.

I can remember a recent occasion when three strangers who I engaged in converstaion all within a period of only two days, said the same thing,

"I'm sick of religion!"

It may be they were referring to rituals and forms of services, or boring messages, or lack-lustre ministers, or stifling religious rules, or sexual abuse, or any number of ugly practices carried out by demonised sinners, under the banner of "Christianity".

The churches have always had the problem similar to that of wordly societies, that is, they are full of sinners. But as one sage put it, *"If you find the perfect church, don't join it, because it won't be perfect any more!"*

Today, Renewal churches have a significant number of damaged people in their meetings, many of whom are on their way to recovery. They are receiving **healing and deliverance, inner cleansing and RESTORATION**- praise the Name of the Lord!

And so today there is a BIG DIFFERENCE between **Religion** and all its man-made showy practices, and **Christianity**. Just read the Gospels of our Lord Jesus Christ and learn of HIS true Christianity. True Christianity is vastly different from religious practice (Jas. 1:27) that is why we need RENEWAL and Renewed churches.

Why, even the Old Testament religious Laws and practices of Israel are, since the Victory of the Cross of Christ, seen as being inspired by the **stoicheia,** that is, **the elemental spirits of the world,** and not the Holy Spirit.

The apostle Paul put it this way:

> *"... **when we were children we were slaves to the elemental spirits of the world.** But when the fullness of time came, God sent forth His Son .. born under the Law so that He might redeem those under the Law.*
>
> *... **now that you have come to know God ... how can you turn again to the weak and poor elemental spirits,** which you again wish to serve a new?*
>
> *You observe days and months and seasons and years.*
>
> *I am afraid for you, that I have laboured among you in vain".*
>
> (Gal. 4:3-11, cf.Col. 2:8,16,20).

Can you imagine that? The enemy (the elemental spirits) used the Old Testament Law so they could CONDEMN the Israelites and, indeed, the whole world (Rom. 2:12,3:19,4:15,5:12-13,20-21).

Praise the Lord, we Christians are no longer under the condemnation of the Law but under God's grace! (Rom. 5:1-2,

20; 6:14) - but if we go back to observing the religious laws[1] of Moses we put ourselves back under the authority and control of the elemental spirits again! God forbid! Many church traditions (Col. 2:8) are a brick wall, instead of being a doorway to our Creator God.

There have been many attempts to explain the difference between Christianity and all other religions in the world. Christians rightly emphasise that **Christ offers the forgiveness of our sins** - a pardon - to those who become His followers and this seems to be unique to the Christian faith. Another enormous difference lies in the definition of Christianity which is described as **God reaching out to man"** (through Jesus Christ) whereas all other religions are based on the gropings of **"man reaching out to God"**. God has succeeded where man has failed.

The Word of God indicates it is impossible for man to find God with His own efforts alone (John 15:5b) hence man-made religions always fall far short of the truth and often end up in spiritism, ancestor-worship and witchcraft.

1.1 CHRISTIAN CELEBRATIONS

Have you noticed how happy the western world is to recognise "Easter" and Christmas? However the recognition is becoming more and more heathen and less and less Christian, which is not surprising.

Most of us have no problem with honouring the birth of Christ on Dec. 25th. So it's the wrong date - so what? At least it's name honours the Christ and His becoming flesh amongst us. Not so with "Easter". Many Christians have

---

1 As distinct from the MORAL laws, which are carried through to the **NEW** Testament.

been telling us that the word "Easter" is a direct reference to a pagan goddess of creation and fertility, and has no Christian meaning at all, hence easter bunnies and eggs. Together with this information we should also note that before and after God told the Hebrews to destroy the shrines and idols of the gods of the nations around them He also instructed them to **not even speak the names of their gods, ever again.** (Exod. 23:13, Josh. 23:7, Psalm 16:4). Apparently to even use the word E....r is to honour this pagan goddess, and as a consequence the emphasis that the New Testament gives the **Crucifixion and Resurrection** of our Lord Jesus Christ is almost completely lost.

The foolishness of applying the name of a pagan goddess to a vital and holy Christian celebration is quite repugnant to informed Christians but not at all repugnant to the secular and pagan society around us. I urge all true disciples of the Lord to not only put Christ back into Christmas but also re-establish the day we celebrate for the Resurrection as **"Resurrection Sunday"**. Let us completely eliminate the alternative pagan word. If you feel you have to use the word E....r, I suggest you put a Y in front of it and make it **Yeaster.** As most Christians know, yeast represents **sin** in the Bible, hence Holy Communion is, or should be, celebrated with **unleavened** bread, that is, bread without yeast. Yeaster is a time when our sins were paid for.

If all this is too much, just stick with **"Good Friday"** and **"Resurrection Sunday",** although even those are questionable. When the Christ comes to reign on earth the words Friday and Sunday will disappear, probably to be replaced by numbering as the 6th and 1st days of the week.

The word Friday honours the wife of the false god Odin, and Sunday honours the sun god – that just show us how steeped in historical paganism we still are.

How does the good Lord put up with us? Praise Him for His forgiveness of our ignorance, indeed ALL our sins, known and unknown.

We will have to find NEW TERMS for the Blood Sacrifice of the Son of God and His Resurrection, in the true Church, at least. The sooner the better.

1.2 NON-CHRISTIAN RELIGIOUS SPIRITS

Australian Christians were shocked at the incineration of **Pastor Graham Staines** with his two children in the family car while on mission in Orissa State, India, during January 1999. The crime was allegedly committed by extreme Hindu radicals, while the whole world knows that sections of Islamic fundamentalism have been butchering Christian communities whenever they think their religion is losing ground.

Religious unclean spirits are among the strongest and most dangerous in existence. This can be seen from the well-known clashes between the Lord Jesus Christ and the Pharisees. Jesus accused them of killing the prophets of old (Matt. 23:29-31,37) and warned His disciples that sincere religious people would want to kill them also (John 16:2).

Spirits that seek to set up gods other than the Christian Godhead are, according to the apostle Paul, idolatrous and religious (Acts 17:16,22). **Unclean spirits, of course, love to control.** They are not concerned with worshipping God through Jesus Christ, but they are interested in mockery, deception and self-advertising, **parading their "spirituality" for the applause of men, and seeking the pre-eminence.** There are, of course, religious spirits controlling every non-Christian religion in the world and I suppose every Christian evangelist and personal-worker has been confronted with the opinion that *"all roads lead to the top of the hill"* According to this universalist theory, **Buddhists** find God their way and **Shintoists** their way, **Christians** their way and **Hindus** their way. Well, other religions may say that all (religious) roads lead to God but the Christian faith does not, because Jesus Christ, the founder of Christianity, made it absolutely clear that He was and is the ONLY way, and this is how Paul presented Him in his message on the subject of "the Unknown God" at Athens (Acts 17:23). ***This direct and only Way to God is to continue until the Day of Judgement*** (Psalm 96:13, Matt. 28:20, Acts 17:30-31), ***so it is clear that future "revelations" and "up-dates" cannot change this truth!***

The Deliverance Ministry brings spectacular confirmation of Jesus' claims. At commands issued in Jesus' Name spirits or demons of any and every non-Christian religion you can name have come spitting, whining and wailing out of people. ***Hindu spirits, Buddhist spirits, Qabbala spirits*** - out they come - all of them - at the Name of **Jesus.** They are no match for His Name or the power of His Holy Spirit. Praise the Lord!

Political Religion

In referring to non-Christian religions and the unclean spirits that inspire them we ought not to leave out a religion that has destroyed the lives of probably **one billion people** last century. That is 1000 x 1000 x 1000 people, consisting of two generations of people belonging to the old **Union of Soviet Socialist Republics**, and one generation of their satellites such as **Bulgaria, Romania**, etc., since World War 2.

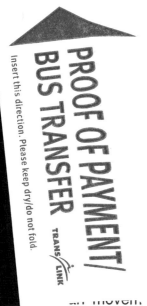

of fifteen republics controlled from
population of around 250 million, but
1ow, thank God. However we are not
munism, that section of the Labour
o violence "whenever necessary", but
nt as a whole. Many people have
ement their religion and are perfectly
it it. They think of it as a religion that
e better - gets things done and not

nd the eighteenth century) it was a
... . inspired by influential men such as
william Wilberforce who attempted to address the terrible
injustices suffered by the poor and slaves alike. Such
injustice bred an equally terrible fury and hatred amongst
the working poor, and soon God was left out. New gods
such as **Marx, Lenin,** and **Engels** replaced the Creator and
a new religion was born, inspired by an anti-Christ spirit,
which preached a gospel of hate. Today we can look back
and say that although members (true believers) of this
religion have seen socialism fail horrendously with enormous
cost in death and poverty to many peoples, many are still
controlled by the religious spirit responsible, because it is
a SPIRITUAL BONDAGE. It therefore lives on today (albeit
under different labels such as humanism, fabianism,
internationalism, social democracy etc.) as a theory (fantasy)
of prosperity which its adherents (slaves) are determined
to foist on all of us and make work somehow, over our dead
bodies if necessary.

When casting out this religious spirit you may need to
include **anger, violence, unbelief, idolatry, hatred** and
murder in your ministering, and perhaps **insanity** as well.
The Labour Movement has only ever been united by force
(tyranny) and fear.

The Labour Movement continues to use the blasphemous banner **"The Unity of Labour is the Hope of the World"** at its conferences, and has done so at least since 1907. Christians who have any understanding of the Word of God in the New Testament will know that **the Lord Jesus Christ is THE HOPE of the World!**

PEARLY GATES

Used with permission of Ian Jones, Pearly Gates Promotions

CHAPTER 2

RELIGIOUS SPIRITS IN THE CHURCHES

Does Christianity also suffer from hidden religious spirits? You had better believe it!

There has always been a life-threatening tension between "religious" people and God's true Christian servants. The Church of the day has even executed saintly great men like **John Hus**, the Bohemian Reformer (1415 A.D.), **Savonarola,** the Italian Reformer (1498 A.D.) - a host of **English** and **French Reformers**, while others like **Martin Luther** escaped plots against their lives. **John Wesley** and his band of preachers suffered violence during the eighteenth century Wesleyan Revival in England, but all this is simply following in the tradition of John the Baptist and, most importantly, our Lord Jesus Christ Himself.

With the revelation of Jesus of Nazareth we have God sending His only Son who declares that *He (alone) is the Way, the Truth and the Life. No one can come to the Father God except through Him* (John 14:6). **This is Christianity** - God reaching out to a lost and helpless mankind through His Son (John 3:16-19) However, in many places the Church has not been built on the foundation of Jesus Christ ALONE, but also on the PAGANISM of resident religions, making a very unhappy mixture indeed.

It is obvious that the activities of unclean religious spirits in the Christian church are often manifested together with the use of the Name of the Lord Jesus Christ. In fact one could say that not only does the use of the Lord's Name NOT guarantee that only the HOLY Spirit is involved but on the contrary, continuous involving of the Name of the Lord Jesus at every opportunity so as to create the impression of holiness, may well be unclean and counter-productive for the Glory of God. It may be serving the glory of men and therefore by definition, and by its fruit, be seen to be unclean. Also spirits of self-righteousness, mockery and ridicule may be involved.

Christian Hebrew prophet and teacher, **Arthur Katz,** reminds us His Name, Jesus, is to be HALLOWED, not thrown around loosely. This should not surprise us because Jesus warned us so strongly about the religiosity of the Pharisees, who *"for a pretence make long prayers"* and *"like to go about in long (religious) robes and have the best seats in the synagogues (churches)"* (Mark 12:38-40, cf. Matt. 23). This religiosity was not simply a problem confined to non-believers because the Lord specifically **warned His disciples** to *"beware of the leaven of the Pharisees"* (Matt.16:6). Such a warning would not be necessary if there was no real danger His followers could be infected by the disease of pharisaism, and we will look at this more closely in chapter 4. Likewise the apostle **Paul** discovered himself in deadly conflict with a **"circumcision party"** in the early church, so that he had to issue the strongest possible warning to the Galatian church to reject their influence (Gal. chapters 2,5).

More recently in our own day the American prophet **J. Leland Earl** published a revelation he received from the Lord:

> *...After this experience the Lord began to deal with me concerning other spirits which are especially troubling the Body of Christ at this time. He showed me two other groups of three each. In the second group are PROUD SPIRITS, **RELIGIOUS SPIRITS,** AND DECEIVING SPIRITS. In the third group are COVETOUS SPIRITS, LUST SPIRITS and LYING SPIRITS.*

These six, plus the three "bitter" spirits (Jealousy, Criticism, Resentment), are the nine kinds of spirits which are especially defiling the Body of Christ and ARE HINDERING THE SAINTS FROM MOVING INTO THEIR FULL INHERITANCE IN CHRIST. Beloved hear me! **The present move of the Spirit of God is primarily to bring cleansing and deliverance from these spirits of the enemy that the saints be no longer hindered.**

I cannot go into all that the Lord has shown me concerning this subject and the relation of His present move to it. But I do know that HE IS RAISING UP AND ANOINTING VESSELS OF HIS CHOOSING TO BE USED IN THIS MINISTRY.

He has also promised KEEN DISCERNMENT, and I know that along with this gift will go the GIFTS OF KNOWLEDGE AND WISDOM, and also MUCH LOVE AND COMPASSION. FOR THIS IS A MINISTRY OF HELP AND DELIVERANCE, NOT OF CONDEMNATION.

There are many saints who are vexed and oppressed by one or more of these spirits and THEY ARE NOT FULLY AWARE OF IT. THEY MAY SENSE THAT SOMETHING IS WRONG, BUT THEY DON'T KNOW WHAT TO DO OR HOW TO GET DELIVERANCE.

The Lord has shown me that the nine spirits mentioned are the very antithesis of the nine fruits of the Spirit mentioned in Gal. 5:22-23. How can the Lord impart love, joy and peace when many saints are experiencing the bitterness of jealousy, criticism and resentment. It is impossible for saints to express genuine long-suffering, gentleness and goodness towards others if there *are PROUD, **RELIGIOUS,** AND DECEIVING SPIRITS AT WORK IN THEIR LIVES.*

There can be very little real fidelity, meekness and self-control evidenced in those who have succumbed to covetous, lust and lying spirits.

Brother Leland has done us a great service in bringing these revelations before us. Please notice that **RELIGIOUS** spirits are grouped with PROUD and DECEIVING spirits, as one would expect.

2.1 OBVIOUS RELIGIOUS SPIRITS

Did you know that the **traditions of men are inspired by demons?**

*Beware lest anyone rob you through philosophy and empty deceit, **according to the tradition of men, according to the elemental spirits**[1] **of the world**, and not according to Christ. (Col. 2:8).*

Did you know that **religious legalism** is **inspired by demons?**

*If you died with Christ from **the elemental spirits of the world** why do you live as if subject to the world's decrees? Do not touch nor taste nor handle **...according to the injunctions and teachings of men...** (Col. 2:20-22).*

These spirits in "Christians" will ALWAYS oppose genuine Holy Spirit Renewal (Acts 7:51), and finally, did you know

---

1   Elemental spirits is translated from the original "stoicheia" which we explain more fully along the way in chapter 4.4

that much **human wisdom** is earthy, soulish and **demonic?** (James 3:15). Please keep these vital spiritual truths alive in your mind as we now look at obvious religious activity.

Some people are so obviously bound up and active with religious spirits that almost anyone in the Renewal movement can discern them. Some sections of the Church are so totally taken over and controlled by them that it is a miracle and a demonstration of the grace of God that anything inspired by the Holy Spirit ever happens! However, as Paul said, *"the Word of God is not bound!"* (1 Tim. 2:9), and *"the Spirit blows where He wills"* (John 3:8).

Some of the more obvious areas that we can see the operation of religious spirits are as follows:

(i)   CLOTHING FOR SERVICES

"...holding the FORM of religion but denying the POWER of it. Avoid these people." (2 Tim. 3:5)

That is, long, "priestly", colourful robes full of symbolism (dare I say superstitious symbolism). Anything that accentuates a priestly, mediatorial class over and above **the priesthood of ALL believers** (1 Peter 2:5, Rev. 1:6, 20:6), and focuses attention on the ministers rather than the Lord is a potential disaster area.

Men who have a hidden need to be the centre of attention and who do not have the ability to get into **"show biz"** may well find themselves attracted to a form of priesthood. Is it any wonder **transvestite spirits** love to get their houses (captives) into a priesthood. They can then prance around the "altar" with great showmanship, in front of a stupefied audience, dressed in glorious apparel (cf. Luke 7:25) and wearing skirts at that! (Deut. 22:5).

Yet others may have sexual problems and hope that drawing near to God as a priest will help them, by means of a life of holiness empowering them to overcome their dark urges.

All of these situations greatly hinder and taint the genuine servants of the Lord who wear skirts only because their training and traditions require it. They find themselves surrounded by those who are in the "priesthood" for all the wrong reasons. It is probably unnecessary for me to add that those with genuine motives (even though theologically flawed) are seriously compromised by the actors around them.

(ii) CHURCH ORNAMENTS AND IMAGES

Back in 1989 Verlie and I visited **Israel** and **the U.K.**. Two things happened relating to images. In **Jerusalem** we used a Muslim tour guide who led us into one of the churches. Up until that time he had shown us various images and icons without emotion but when we came to a statue (three dimensional image) of the virgin Mary with a sad face, he passionately implored us to gaze upon her (its) countenance.

Later in London we visited **St. Paul's Cathedral** and again our guide became emotional. "Look what they did!" he cried out, pointing to many figurettes with damaged faces and bodies.

He was referring to the **iconoclasts (image breakers)** who went around smashing idols and icons during the biblical **Reformation** of the **16th Century**. I looked (as he requested) and quietly rejoiced!

Most of us know about the **1st and 2nd Commandments** from the **Law of Moses**. They read:

> *You shall have no other gods before me. You shall not make any graven image, or any likeness of anything that is in heaven above, or in the earth beneath, or in the water under the earth: You shall not bow down to them, nor serve them: for I the Lord your God am a jealous God, visiting the iniquity of the fathers upon the children to the third and fourth generation of those who hate me; and showing mercy to thousands of those who love me, and keep my commandments.*
>
> *Exod. 20:3-6*

One might ask why the Lord is concerned about the MAKING of images when He also commands us not to bow down and worship them? Is it not sufficient to instruct us not to worship them? Can we not make images for purposes other than worship? For decoration perhaps, or to satisfy our creative skills or to enjoy?

Quite obviously the good Lord knows how vulnerable we are and how superstitious *(religious, demon-fearing - Acts 17:22)* we can get. It is so easy to "cross the line" in spiritual things and find ourselves chained to something. For example some men can grow long and luxuriant hair which gets a lot of attention. To suggest that it be cut short (cf. 1 Cor. 11:14) for any reason can be tantamount to starting World War III.

Clearly if we are forbidden to MAKE graven images (no matter what the reason) in the first place we cannot then be deceived into giving them undue attention or affection (*follow, serve, worship* - Deut. 8:19) and get ourselves into BIG trouble!

It may surprise many Christians to learn that this matter of images in the Church has been a tumultuous one throughout early church history, with different leaders (Emperor Leo III and Pope Gregory II) contradicting each other, and much bloodshed.

Clever excuses[2] for present day images such as fabricated by the eighth century church cannot justify such rebellion.

The Media is not particularly known for its support of Christianity, but they are often "kindred spirits" with **religiosity** and **churchianity.**

When they came to "my" church, **St. Michael's, Surry Hills (Sydney),** to cover the outbreak of deliverance many years ago, on what did they want to focus their cameras? You've guessed it! Stone walls, gloomy interior, stained glass windows, (two dimensional images) and me sitting in the choir stalls with the old organ behind me.

Artwork: Tim Field- used by permission

---

2   See Appendix A

That is how people see the historic church, largely because the Media often present Christianity today as (unclean) religion, dead as a dodo! To be fair, they don't know how else to present Christian matters visually. I suggest filming a great Renewal worship meeting is the way.

Mournful, old, decrepit, anachronistic, dark, musty, reeking of death and the religious (spirit). Although there may be plenty of numinous[3] from familiar and ancestral spirits, there is not much hint of the **HOLY** Spirit in some historic church buildings, except the presence of a sparrow or a church mouse created by God (Psalm 84:3), There is plenty to indicate "religion".

Don't be surprised when earthquakes and earth tremors demolish these churches!

(iii) CONDUCT OF SERVICES

What value is **bowing** to other robed figures - and the Cross, **turning** to the east, **chanting** and **genuflecting? Processions** may possibly be free of religious activity, depending on the hearts of those involved. I have usually found them a great temptation to indulge in pomp and self-importance but **sometimes** have succeeded in keeping a pure heart, I think! However there can be a temporary closeness and warmth in praise while passing through a genuinely worshipping assembly.

Renewal/Charismatic Input

While we can agree that Charismatic meetings are just as vulnerable to religious spirits as many traditional services, we need to be bold enough to allow the Holy Spirit to sup-

---

3 Feelings of spiritual presence

ply individual gifting to worshippers, even at the risk of making public mistakes.

For example, public tongues should be interpreted (1 Cor. 14:5-12, 19, 27-28) if not by others then by the one who spoke in tongues (1 Cor. 14:13). Likewise with prophecies which should be weighed by others (1 Cor. 14:29, 32). Supernatural activities of the Holy Spirit should not just be received by worshippers with the mouth wide open but checked for genuineness. (1 John 4:1). It is not an unforgivable sin to make mistakes – everyone does – but it is wrong not to check the source of the "gifting" and CORRECT where necessary.

The leadership of Renewal churches that have traditional, historic roots usually tread quite carefully into public ministries such as healing and deliverance. Yes, changes can cause division (Luke 12:51, John 7:43) and Yes, Pastors can feel "out-of-their-depth" and alarmed. This is where they are being tested as to Who is Head of the Church (Eph. 1:22, Col. 1:18) and do they really TRUST the leading of the Holy Spirit? The caring pastor has to look past the hype, the exaggeration and the errors and get the regulation of Holy Spirit gifts RIGHT! (1 Cor. 14).

A Deception to Avoid

There are some pastors who have settled for a low-key charismatic input into their meetings and are quite genuine and up-front about where they stand, whether it be right or wrong. However there are others who try to be "all things to all men" and practice a little deception.

It goes something like this:

1. He resists Renewal and preaches against it because it cuts across his traditions, and Christians in Renewal make so many mistakes!

2. After a short period of attempted adjustments by both sides, those who have been touched by the Holy Spirit leave to join a Pentecostal style church. This can leave quite a gap in his church's workforce.

3. Over a period of time the minister sees his flock diminishing and gets desperate to (i) stop the drain away to Pentecost, and (ii) have departures replaced by newcomers.

4. The minister begins to make Renewal gestures and noises. He brings in some worship music from the movement, with guitars and keyboard ("That seems safe"). He talks about the Holy Spirit but always points out the dangers of "going overboard", which can be quite a fair criticism but can also cloak negativity.

5. He introduces healing prayer, perhaps once a month (God help the sick who may have to wait for the set day to come around!).

6. With Renewal music, his healing line and his messages on the Holy Spirit he is now thought of as a Charismatic by some of his patient and trusting flock, who believe their church is on the move. He keeps some of his young people and he holds his loyal senior people. He keeps his hierarchy happy. All seems well.

There may be just a few little things wrong with all of that. He may be a fraud. He may have no intention of moving ahead with the Spirit of God. He is giving his people false hope under false pretences. God knows his heart and that he is motivated, not by seeking the perfect will of God for himself and his people but by numerical and financial survival. He may still be a traditionalist and a boot-licker of the men who run the system and not a true servant of the Lord. The demise of his congregation seems to have been averted, but it is really only temporary. The Lord will not leave that flock under a deceiver for long. Other assemblies with apostolic vision and power will soon be birthed nearby and God's hungry people shall be satisfied (Ps. 63:5, Matt. 5:6).

How do you know who is a counterfeit or fraudulent charismatic minister?

There are probably many ways but I can suggest three indicators that may help:

(i)   He allows worship songs to be sung only once. Genuine charismatics know that people have to stop singing with their heads and begin worshipping with their (human) spirits (John 4:24). This usually involves singing a worship song more than once - perhaps several times - as the WORDS sink into the spirit. Many with **intellectual** faith find this quite difficult, even irritating.

(ii) He never gives the REAL Head of the Church the opportunity to break into the meeting with a Word of prophecy for His people.

(iii) He is not interested in having deliverance ministry in his assembly, notwithstanding the Word of God's command to Christians to be cleansed (2 Cor. 7:1, James 4:8 etc.). Somehow he reads the words *"psychiatrist"*, *medicine* and *"drugs"* into the New Testament - a strange miracle indeed!

Change your church? Long ago I would have said not to change your church unless you really felt a strong leading to do so, but now, when most churches have had many opportunities to move with God, I would say:

"If you can't change your church - change your church!"

- especially if your Pastor/Minister/Priest continues to believe, and persists in believing, against ALL the evidence, that a Christian cannot have a demon.

CHOIR and ALTAR BOYS

You know the Word of God tells us that *God is Spirit and those who worship Him MUST worship Him in spirit and in truth* (John 4:24). I take that to mean that **only worship by the human spirit of a person is acceptable to God**. Not head worship or soulish (natural) worship (1 Cor. 2:14) by a person, but **worship in (by or with) the human spirit.**

That means, of course, the human spirit must be BORN AGAIN (John 3:3-5). It was once dead in trespasses and sin but when you become a Christian your spirit is made alive again (Eph. 2:1-5), and therefore enabled to worship God as He wants, spiritually!

Now if it is true that only BORN AGAIN Christians are able to offer God acceptable worship (and this is the teaching of the Lord Jesus Christ) then what are we doing getting little **choir boys** or famous **big name singers** to sing parts in **Handel's "Messiah"???**

If they love the Lord - that's fine, but does anybody bother to check? I was myself a choir boy for many years, but I didn't know the Lord and nobody checked me out with the love of Christ.

When you listen to a choir have you noticed that, although the boy sopranos sing sweetly it is rarely in, with or by the spirit? However as soon as the adults come in, the Spirit of God comes in with their spirits and the whole worship is lifted!

That is not to say we should not use choir boys - their Christian training is important. However they need counselling, prayer and nurturing in the Lord as much as anyone else.

The same principle applies to altar boys, most of whom seem to backslide out of the Faith when older.

Think about it.

(iv) CHRISTIAN SYMBOLISM

Almost all contrived ritual and symbolism in Church services springs from the activity of religious spirits, not the Holy Spirit. You will find nothing to support many of these activities in the New Testament of our Lord Jesus Christ. They are distractions and diversions which focus human attention on themselves, rather than the object/person they are supposed to symbolise.

So much Church symbolism is attention-seeking showmanship! In the New Testament I see only four key symbols for Christians to use

(i)   **Unleavened Bread** *represents* the Lord's Body in Holy Communion.

(ii)   **The fruit of the vine** (not necessarily wine) *represents* the Lord's Blood. (Mark 14:25)

(iii)   **Water** represents the Holy Spirit in Baptism. (Acts 2:38)

(iv)   **Oil** represents the Holy Spirit in Healing (James 5:14).

There is nothing gaudy, flashy or colourful about any of these symbols. In New Testament times they were everyday items easily available to all and probably found in every Hebrew home, yet these common items **represent** the Lord Jesus and His Spirit! Do you perceive the wisdom of the Lord in this?

If you have been taught that the bread/wafer and wine used in the Mass or Holy Communion **LITERALLY** become The Body and Blood of our Lord, this contradicts the figurative, representative and memorial nature of **the Bread of Affliction** as presented in the **Jewish Passover**, which is the origin and basis of our **Christian Passover**, often known today as the Mass or Holy Communion.

Please note also the *memorial* and *representative* nature of the Cup:

> *"This Cup is the New Covenant in/with/by My blood."*
> *Luke 22:20, 1 Cor. 11:25)*

There is no way the Cup Jesus used was/is LITERALLY the New Covenant. "Covenant" means a binding legal document or agreement, not a drinking vessel, and He is speaking figuratively:

"This Cup (its contents) REPRESENTS the New Covenant (sealed/obtained) in/with/by My blood."

I believe a religious spirit is at work encouraging many Christians to feed on Christ in their **stomachs** and not their **hearts.** Jesus' words are SPIRITUAL and not intended to be taken literally (John 6:51-56,63), but figuratively.

Sickness

Getting all this wrong can have disastrous consequences.

The apostle Paul warns us that to profane the Body and Blood of the Lord is a doorway to sickness, and even (early) death.

"For anyone who eats and drinks without discerning (spiritually) the body eats and drinks judgment to himself. Therefore many among you are weak (sick) and feeble, and some sleep (have died)."

(1 Cor. 11:29-30).

Many ministers have tried to exercise a healing ministry but have become disheartened when their prayers for a sufferer have not been answered. They have expected instant, or at least, speedy healings and when neither of those things happen, they give up, thinking they do not have the necessary gifting from the Holy Spirit.

In fact *"failures"* should teach us much. If we REALLY believe the Word of God is true for today we need to search in every way possible for the reason(s) why we "fail". For example, do you know of anyone who has led a sufferer in repentant prayer for wrong, false, flippant, fleshly, idolatrous, thoughtless, careless and even profane participation in Holy Communion??? No? Neither do I, outside of our own ministry.

Now, back to Christian symbolism.

Unleavened bread and the **fruit of the vine** *represent* His body and His blood - given and shed for us upon Calvary's Cross - not gold crosses and ornate crucifixes. Neither do we need long robes in the market places, or even in Church, **IF** our hearts are filled with the Holy Spirit. Christianity is not about visible externals. Man looks on the outward appearance, but God looks on the heart (1 Sam. 16:7). When we emphasise visible, external symbols it robs us from focussing on the Holy Spirit within us. They will know us by our love (John 13:35) and the FRUIT of the indwelling Spirit in our lives (Matt. 7:15-20). These fruit are SPIRITUAL, although they reveal themselves physically.

(v) PRAYER

Many evangelicals would be surprised to learn they are highly religious. They think of High Churchmanship or Catholic-style ritual as religious because these emphasise external symbolism (shadows) rather than the substance which is the Spirit of Christ (Col. 2:16-17). They themselves may be immersed in **intellectualism**, where they are comfortable because they are "in control," but fear the gifts and the leading of the Holy Spirit because then the Lord is in Control. Sometimes they are locked into ancient hymns and ancient tunes rather than Scripture set to modern melodies: they are locked into **Prayer Book services with read prayers** because they do not trust the flock to pray proper, doctrinally accurate prayers, forgetting that the Lord looks upon the heart. It is usually man that is offended by confused or inaccurate or poorly phrased prayers. The Lord Himself looks upon the **heart** and judges and answers accordingly - not just our spoken words alone but the cry of our hearts.

I remember when the Diocese in which I was serving the Lord wanted to break out of the pattern of the minister being the "one-man-band plus Australian Prayer Book" syndrome, and decided to encourage prayers in services by people other than the Minister. This revolutionary, brave experiment began by authorising certain people of good repute to say prayers as well as the minister.

At a given signal from the minister they would rise up from their pew, walk to the appropriate microphone at the front, and read out a pre-written prayer from a slip of paper. It all sounds so ludicrous and artificial now but at the time few thought it so. Apparently unprepared or extempore prayer by whoever desired to pray was considered too dangerous.

Such human precautions and checks may seem justified in the matter of public prayers but when the result is the locking OUT of the Holy Spirit's leading to the individual Christian to pray whatever prayer burden has been laid upon his or her heart, then I say that good order and decency has degenerated into stultifying legalism. I say that the price for such "decency" is TOO HIGH, and although such attempt at prayer communion with the Most High may have been expressed in truth, it may not have been in Spirit; that is, from the human spirit, led by the Holy Spirit, communing with God who is Spirit (John 4:24). Extempore, ad-libbed prayers do NOT have to mean lack of order or decency or discipline, but they DO mean that the Holy Spirit can get into the meeting and lead human hearts.

And if someone prays what we think is a rotten prayer, we don't have to say AMEN. We can trust the good Lord to deal with it HIS way!

The stranglehold of the religious spirit can be measured to some degree by the insistence of some Christians in holding to every detail of printed rituals for worship.

For example, a small number of Roman Catholics continue to insist on holding services in Latin. Way back in 1970 Vatican Council II authorised and changed its services into the language of the people, and this especially blessed English speaking members.

After all, the Word of God tells us that languages in foreign/ unknown tongues have to be interpreted **so the Church of God can be edified** (1 Cor. 14:13).

Now I see that the Prayer Book Society in Australia is advertising itself. No one denies the Prayer Book contains many wonderful prayers to read to the Lord, and it is a rich source of inspiration, but its function should be a reservoir of source material to be used **at the discretion of the user.**

No one who has publicly committed themselves to their denomination's Articles of Religion (Statement of Faith) and/or been ordained should be obligated to use it.

We should also add that having a formal liturgy with prayers read from a book, and an Order of Service to be followed by minister and worshippers, has NOT prevented significant sections[4] of the historic churches moving away from the Word of God and into heresy.

Faithful Preparation Still Desirable

There is no doubt that for centuries evangelicals have settled for a level of Reformation in church services which, although a vast improvement on pre-Prayer Book days prior to 1549 AD, nevertheless failed to rise to the kind of worship which Jesus says is absolutely necessary, combining TRUTH AND the inspiration, moment to moment, of the HOLY SPIRIT.

If the concept of extempore or "open" prayers causes a frown or sends shudders up any Christian leader's spine then it may be time for them to get rid of their religiosity. The good Lord has given us the Renewal Movement in this twentieth century so that the Body of Christ can learn to be led by the Spirit in services and meetings, and learn to WORSHIP in the spirit/Spirit.

---

4   The battles, both theological and legal, between the various traditional streams within the Anglican church spring quickly to mind, namely Evangelical, Middle, High and Anglo Catholic.

I am not suggesting there should be no preparation for services or meetings. Nor am I suggesting there should be no format or order, or earlier choosing and **preparation of worship songs, prayers and messages**, even with prayer and fasting.

However any such prepared material must be held together gently and sensitively, so that the Holy Spirit can FLOW in - without having to BREAK in! Those who lead meetings must be spiritually fluid enough to change the program, to allow the expected (a word of prophecy?) or the unexpected (a demonised man creating some drama down the back?) to happen, and respond to that happening as the Holy Spirit leads (cf. Mark 1:21-28).

Life, Not Death

Having read prayers in historic church situations for many years, doing "my best" by the grace of God to make them alive and meaningful, I can say that, beautiful as many of them are, they often miss the mark, because **the Kingdom of God consists not in word (talk) but in Power** (1 Cor. 4:20), and the Holy Spirit is inhibited from LEADING the prayers.

What is the value of a Prayer Book containing various froms of service? I suggest it:

(i)   helps the prayerless to pray
(ii) provides basic structures to meet special human needs
(iii) provides source material (e.g. Scriptures) suitable for special occasions
(iv) reveals the Christian faith and doctrine of its users.

All of this means the Prayer Book can be used as a very helpful source from which ministers can draw, but to insist on its legalistic and confining use is to contradict the headship of Christ over His church and the need to listen to, and obey, the leading of the Holy Spirit in EVERY assembly (Rom. 8:14).

Prayer MUST come from the human heart and born again spirit, or it is just a religious exercise, as bad as saying prayers by numbers (1,2,3....). I don't need to tell you who or what inspires such religiosity.

With services that are strictly read from a prayer book the best one can hope for is that parts of the service will be inspired for the participants, but we should not expect the Holy Spirit to take control, except in very unusual situations.. *"The letter kills, the Spirit gives LIFE!"* (2 Cor. 3:6). The choice is READ prayers or LED prayers! DEAD prayers or LIVING prayers!

(vi) RELIGIOUS CONVERSATION

It is probably obvious to most Christians that the clearest exposure of a "hidden" unclean religious spirit, outside of church building services and meetings is - ordinary conversation. I once had a very keen, Bible-trained Deaconess on my staff at **St. Michael's, Sydney,** but-oh the vocabulary!

Every conversation was couched in the most syrupy, gooey, pious, religious language. It was rather like the script of a slow-moving Hollywood religious epic (not, I hasten to add, on the life of Jesus, which have generally been done as well as one could expect).

Some people pray like that. They produce a different language from the normal with plenty of *thees*, *thys* and *thous.* They even produce a different voice, especially when they prophesy. In very severe cases the language is always couched in such a way as to make sure you know you are talking to a full-on, mature, spiritual giant. Such Christians do not often manifest the genuine joy of the Lord. How can they? The religious spirit has them in chains and they are more likely to carry associated problems of legalism, and perhaps mournfulness. Their personalities are NOT a good witness which will attract people to the Lord Jesus, but rather the opposite.

(vii) SUPERSTITION

Superstition can sometimes be demonstrated by the Sign of the Cross[5] being made by someone. I normally have mixed feelings when I see a small cross hung around someone's neck, if only because it reveals that person to have an awareness of spiritual things and probably God-fearing.

Even if a cross or crucifix is worn as an act of superstition, hoping for Godly protection, it gives me the opportunity to speak about faith and Christ. When I ask "Are you a Christian?" they usually respond "Catholic"- but at least we are TALKING!

You may remember the apostle Paul was deeply offended by the idolatry in Athens, but used one altar inscribed "To An Unknown God" to launch his message:

---

5. The Sign of the Cross is made by drawing the right hand from forehead to chest, and then from shoulder to shoulder. Western churches usually make the cross-stroke from left to right, and Eastern churches from right to left. It is often used when people want something from the Lord – a blessing, protection, victory in battle or sporting events etc.

"What therefore you worship as unknown,
This I proclaim to you.....!!!"

Acts 17:23

People wear a cross for many reasons and I would suspect the larger and more obvious it is, the more "religious" they are, depending on gadgets and visible symbols to protect them rather than the invisible blood of the Passover Lamb (Exod. 12:12-14, 1 Cor. 5:7) which should be prayed (and spiritually sprayed) over us (believers) at the beginning of each day.

Although there was **once** a mystery about God He has now revealed Himself through His only begotten Son (John 14:7-11, Eph. 3:8-11, Heb. 1:1-3). He has now revealed to us His character, attributes and power. He has made Himself known through His Word and by His Spirit. Indeed - wonder of wonders! - He has even made us temples of His Holy Spirit and dwells WITHIN EVERY BORN AGAIN CHRISTIAN. We are in Him and He is in us! (John 3:3-8, 1 Cor. 3:16-17, 6:19, John 14:7, 20,23).

Thus He has revealed Himself to us in a very personal way. He has revealed His person, His salvation and His will. He has even revealed the enemy, and how He has legally defeated him (Col. 2:15, 1 John 3:8). He has dispelled darkness with light (John 1:4-5), and shares an intimate friendship (confides) in those who fear Him (Psalm 25:14). Therefore **superstition** can only thrive amongst Christians where there is false teaching (doctrines of demons - 1 Tim. 4:1) and ignorance of the Word of God. (cf. 2 Cor. 2:10-11).

During his preaching at the Areopagus in Athens **Paul** began tactfully but truthfully, declaring that he perceived the Athenians were very **superstitious** or **religious** (Acts 17:22). The word means literally **"demon-fearing"**, and understood to mean **"gods-fearing"**, as indeed demons and gods often mean the same things in Bible passages and in tribal societies today. So when a person says they are superstitious it usually means they are very sensitive to the activities of the spirit world, especially the unclean spirit world and its rule of fear over mankind. The bottom line is that **superstitious behaviour within the Christian church is a very clear and obvious indication of the activity of religious (and other) spirits.**

(viii) ANGER

I have often been amazed at the manifestation of anger that springs out of the most unlikely people at times.

At a Rural Deanery meeting in 1974 I was asked to speak on the Deliverance Ministry. After 15 minutes one usually quiet and highly respected minister could not contain himself any longer. *"Where do you get the term deliverance from anyway?"* he snarled, his eyes popping with anger.

When I calmly told him it came from the Lord's prayer, he just glared at me, speechless. We could easily have enjoyed an effective deliverance session right there in the middle of the Deanery.

We know that many of the wars that have erupted in the latter half of this twentieth century have been over religious matters, especially when we understand that Communism and Socialism are religions. Things can get to a place where hate just takes over and human rights are "forgotten" but I believe we are going to find that, more and more, people's religious differences are going to cause divisions and bloodshed all over the world, and the deception known as **multi-culturalism** (in reality idolatrous POLYTHEISM, and therefore inspired by the anti-Christ spirit -1 John 4:1-6) lead to civil wars within nations.

As a theological student I belonged to a group of Christians that was very confident they had most of the answers, and at least twice as many answers as any other Christians. Then came the **Charismatic** or **Renewal movement** and evangelicals suddenly found themselves on the defensive. On three separate occasions my evangelical friends became very angry with me when I parted from the traditional line of thinking. I found that very interesting, because normally when an evangelical finds himself in a theological dispute, he welcomes debate, confident he has the truth. He will debate long and lovingly to win the day because he believes he is in a winning position and cannot be shaken.

However when HIS traditions are also exposed by the Spirit of God and he is put on the defensive, watch out for the anger of the religious spirit!

CHAPTER 3

MORE PERSONAL RELIGIOSITY

Even more obvious as the activity of religious spirits is the hypocritical behaviour of some people who claim to be Christians. I remember an acquaintance expressing horror at the conduct of a business "friend". My acquaintance was owed quite a lot of money by his "friend", who had also cheated him in another business deal. So when this "friend" asked him to make a donation to his Church charity he said to me "How is that for a two-faced hypocrite? He cheats me and then wants me to help his church!"

Did you know that the Word of God says that this will be normal in the last days (of this Age)? Men will be:

> *lovers of themselves, lovers of money,*
> *boasters, proud, blasphemers,*
> *disobedient to parents,*
> *ungrateful, unholy, unloving, unforgiving,*
> *slanderers, without self-control, brutal,*
> *despisers of good, traitors, headstrong,*
> *haughty, lovers of pleasure rather than God,*
> *HAVING A FORM OF GODLINESS, BUT DENYING*
> *ITS POWER, ... always learning and never able to*
> *come to the knowledge of the truth (2 Tim. 3:1-7).*

What an incredible mixture of religiosity and evil!

Here is the largest list of **the works of the flesh** recorded in the New Testament, even larger than the well-known list in Galatians 5:19-21, and one of its longest phrases tells us that **holding to religious forms as a kind of counterfeit, powerless Christianity will be a feature of the End Time!**

The Word of God encourages us to avoid altogether the kind of people who hold the FORM of religion but deny the POWER of it (2 Tim. 3:2-5). Note carefully. The Word doesn't say that we should fellowship with the FORMAL religionists and avoid the effective ministries with God's POWER, but just the opposite! You will realise that, generally speaking, today's situation is that the FORMAL religionists of the traditional church denominations are busy warning the people of God NOT to be drawn into the Renewal movement of God's POWER and so they expressly contradict the Word, that they may keep their tradition and (hopefully) their people (Mark 7:9).

So much for **obvious manifestations** of religious spirits.

3.1   SOME MAJOR PROBLEMS

I would now like to focus attention on the more **subtle, hidden religious spirits** that have infested the Christian Church, home and society for centuries. It is the Lord's time to expose them in order that the Church might be cleansed! Here are some areas against which we need to be on our guard.

(i)   SELF RIGHTEOUS DOGMATISM

A precious Christian sister was overjoyed to visit our Deliverance and Restoration program and after two or three meetings wrote:

"Thank you for your wonderful and blessed ministry. May the Lord increase the years on you both and continue the awesome work that He's chosen you two for. Hopefully (we will) bring more souls for cleansing so ... they receive full salvation."

Suddenly she left the program and we learnt the obstacle was Verlie getting stuck into **self-righteous spirits** and commanding them out of those in the meeting. I remember how she really hammered them, in Jesus' Name. It may not have affected many of those present but it certainly affected our sister and that was the last we saw of her.

Self-righteousness is, unfortunately, a common problem with full-on, maturing Christians, and makes us appear as mean-spirited.

Many people with religious spirits, and that is most people, Christians included, truly believe they have a quality of holiness or godliness in the right way. They are like **Job's three friends** who meant well but ended up having to apologise to Job because they got it WRONG! (Job 42:7-10).

All their religious counsel (29 chapters of it) was not the mind of God in this case (cf. Isa. 55:8-11). Without realising it **some have replaced the righteousness of God with a righteousness of their own** (Rom. 10:3); they believe they are righteous and "holier than thou" (Isa. 65:5), because **"religious" people are hyper-religious and self-righteous.** They naturally and genuinely believe their attitude and approach is right, and others are WRONG or less spiritual. Therefore they enjoy this form of uncleanness. It is not like beastly lust or violence or treachery for which it is easy to feel guilt, shame and condemnation. Religiosity carries a very strong sense of righteousness and *it is therefore most difficult for people with this form of problem to:*

    (i) **recognise that it IS unclean, not holy, and**

    (ii) **WANT to change**

Self-righteousness gives people a sense of **self esteem** and **worth,** and also **power** and **superiority** over other "lesser" mortals and not everyone wants to lose these "advantages".

It is very often a spirit which enters after earlier experiences of rejection and inferiority by way of compensation for the lack of human love and attention. When a child or person fails to obtain sufficient attention and acceptance to meet their emotional needs, they may turn to the Lord as the One who is always there, always supportive and comforting and who fills the needs not met by the human family. Thus it becomes so easy to create a set of religious exercises by means of which one is supported and sustained, while rejection and inadequacy are over-ruled with a new sense of self-esteem founded on spirituality. Hence the people likely to have religious spirits in the normal Christian assembly will often be found amongst those who truly love the Lord and are generally considered mature in the faith. However this love of the Lord can be mixed with a desire to be recognised and accepted by other Christians, similar to **Diotrephes'** problem of seeking pre-eminence (3 John 9).

(ii)   WORLDLY NOTIONS OF RIGHTEOUSNESS

Religious spirits may also enter during "brain-washing" by educational facilities such as High School or University. In studying the Humanities old historic injustices are regurgitated, provoking anger at man's inhumanity to man. This anger creates a receptive and fertile hot-bed for socialistic notions[1] of "equality" and "justice" to find root. So

---

1   The socialist's view of equality is a totally non-discriminatory world where everyone eats the same, dresses the same, lives in the same style house, drives the same make of car. Factors such as integrity, industry, study, intelligence, laziness, immorality, blessings and curses do not count for much in their systems. They even label you "sexist" or "chauvinist" if you distinguish between men and women! And, of course, Christianity is a no no!

much of this historical information is inaccurate or at the very least warped, fragmented and biased presentations of what really happened because, very simply, historians were not present at the events they describe. They piece together fragments of information from documents and diaries etc., and then weave their "histories" together with a lot of imagination based on probabilities. The "flesh" they put on the "bones" is not always (seldom?) right (cf. 1 Cor. 15:39?).

"History is bunk!"
        Henry Ford (July 1919)

"All our ancient history... is no more than accepted fiction"
        Voltaire (in Jeannot et Colin)

"(Read to me) anything but history, for history must be false!"
        Sir Robert Walpole to his son.

We are not, of course, denying historical facts such as the assassination of American President Abraham Lincoln in 1865 A.D., but question the MOTIVES thought to be be-hind the actions of many historical figures. Why did they do this? – Or that? Even their spoken or written comments which sound righteous or reasonable may hide deeper, hid-den, selfish motives in their soul. Only they really know the truth.

Did you ever watch that television documentary on the causes of World War I? I lost count of the (possible) reasons put for-ward by one historian.

Historians are required to INTERPRET facts; which is why they so often differ from each other. They are like three preachers who present three different messages from the same Bible passage, according to their individual bias and interpretation. Consequently religious spirits inspiring Marxist, Communist or Socialist notions find easy access into the hearts of angry and idealistic young men and women students, especially during tertiary education. So it should not surprise us to discover that such political movements become religions, and even Communism which has decimated nations and millions of people for nearly a century, as we have already said, still holds sway deep in the hearts of many.

Why? It is a heart/soul thing. It is spiritual. **It is a spiritual bondage that is religious** (as so many of them freely admit), and therefore it is one of the most difficult chains to break. **Usually it is only death or Jesus who can help us change our religion.** Even atheists (those who believe there is no God) are religious. In denying the existence of gods or a supreme God they elevate themselves into that position. They recognise no being higher than man, and therefore they view man (themselves) as God. They set themselves up in His place and serve themselves in a man-centred religion.

(iii) WE LIKE BEING RELIGIOUS

The major difficulty remains. We know and like our religion. Most of us would rather die than change this part of us. Verlie and I have been in Deliverance work for more than thirty years and during that time people have cried out for help and removal of a huge variety of unclean spirits of fear, infirmity etc. etc., but **no one has ever come to us and requested deliverance from their religious spirits!!**

We do not perceive our religious spirits as being a problem to us. Indeed Christians think they are being led by the Spirit of God, and so gain a sense of security from them (e.g.

revering statues, paintings of Jesus, crucifixes). Such spirits make one feel important and right (dogmatic) and enable us to "correct" other lesser mortals.

They make us formidable opponents, so why would we want to lose them? If we are self centred we will NOT want to lose them, but if we are truly disciples of the Lord, seeking the fulness of GOD'S Spirit and HIS Will for our lives, we have no choice.

Verlie and I have lost at least two very dear friends through religious spirits. Verlie prayed and fasted three weeks for one sister, but she didn't want to lose them and so they stayed put. Many other victories were obtained during those three weeks - by people who WANTED to be set free but NOT the Christian who would not listen. It can be very difficult to tell a brother or sister in Christ that the spirit leading them is NOT the Holy Spirit, but unclean. Then it becomes a battle of trust. Will they continue to trust their OWN judgement, or will they trust (accept) ours?

The battle for their cleansing is won or lost right here!

Religious Presumption

"You shall not put the Lord your God to the test."
(Matt. 4:7, Deut. 6:16).

You might remember this response of Jesus to the second temptation of the devil recorded in Mattew's gospel:

"Then the devil took Him (Jesus) into the Holy City and stood Him on the wing (highest balcony) of the Temple and said to Him 'If you are the Son of God, cast yourself down, for it is written, To His angels He will give command concerning You, and on

(their) hands they will bear You, lest You strike Your foot against a stone." (Matt. 4:5-6)

Christians fall for this temptation all the time! Just change the words "the Son of God" to "a Christian". It then reads –If you are a Christian just do this or that. You will be perfectly safe because God's angels will protect you.It might be dangerous for others, but not you.

On this understanding, of course, no Christian need ever die in battle. There will be times, of course, that believers are miraculously brought through **"the valley of the shadow of death"** (Psa.23:4), such as the shepherd boy David over the giant warrior Goliath, and Sergeant Alvin York who with seven survivors, triumphed over 157 enemy front – line soldiers in 1918. York had a sense of the presence and protection of the Lord but he never spoke of it in any religious, self - promotional way.

A co-worker surprised me (and others) by declaring he and his family never locked the front door or the windows of their home. At a time of many break and enter burglaries we told him of our concern, to which he replied:

"Ah, you haven't seen the four angels stationed over each corner of the house!"

He was right, I had not. I don't know if they were really there or not. All I knew was that he was not taking simple, basic security precautions and was asking for trouble. **It is when we have done all (we can do) we can stand in the Faith Position** (Eph. 6:13).

As Verlie has often said, when you are parking your car trust the Lord and lock the doors! Remember that **presumption is sin** (Deut. 17:11-13, Psa. 19:13, 2 Pet.

2:10), so hang onto *"All things work together for good to those who love the Lord and are called according to His purpose"* (Rom.8:28).

But

"Do not put the Lord your God to the test!".

(iv) BE CAREFUL WHAT YOU SAY!

Following on from the subject of Religious Presumption we would like to make another point with which you may disagree. Having a continuous pastoral responsibility over an elderly saint we parted company on one occasion with the words "Take care!" I received a broadside of words (rebuke) back indicating that she didn't need to take care because the Lord (or an angel) was watching over her, and my words were negative and without faith. Words expressing compassion and encouraging alertness (watch and pray) were interpreted to be faithless.

On another occasion a sister explained to Verlie how someone had steered a shopping trolley over her toes. Verlie responded with "O you poor darling!" The word "poor" in this context expressed concern for possible physical damage, and pain, but the compassion was rejected with the person denying they were poor.

These are extremes to which some Renewal Christians have carried their "positive thinking". Verlie and I think the following Scripture is still valid:

Blessed be the God and Father of our Lord Jesus Christ, the Father of mercies and God of all comfort; who comforts us in all our affliction so that we may be able to comfort those who are

*in any affliction with the comfort with which we
ourselves are comforted by God.*

*For just as the sufferings of Christ are ours in
abundance, so also our comfort is abundant
through Christ.*

(2 Cor. 1:3-5).

Full On for the Lord!

I used to think that the closer I drew to God the more
successful I would be in my ministry. I thought that all true
Christian people would see how close I was to God and
they would be attracted to the Christ in me (i.e. in my work
or church or whatever) because they would respond to the
REALITY of God in Christ, in me, But I had not fully
understood what Jesus meant when He said that He
repelled many men because He was the Light and when
men saw Him as the Light they would WITHDRAW from
Him because their deeds were evil. (John 2:23-25, 3:19-
21). Now that may be understandable regarding the men of
the world, who have not known God the Father or His Son,
Jesus Christ, but why would CHRISTIAN men and women
be repelled by meetings or services where the presence
and power of God was very strong, or where His REALITY
was powerfully confirmed through miracles of healings and
deliverances? I remember one woman who came up to me
after a **Deliverance and Restoration** meeting and said
**"I've been to a lot of Renewal meetings but that was
the most powerful meeting I have ever attended!"** It
disappointed us that we never saw her again, or others who
have said the same.

Another deeply committed Christian wept with joy after his
first visit with us. **"It's what I've been looking for!"** We didn't
see him again either!

Another woman told us *"I'm full-on for the Lord".* Our hearts went clunk! - when we heard that because we knew the Accuser would take her words before the Throne of God and get permission to test her spiritual condition (Rev. 12:10). She barely lasted one meeting. Another young man said the same thing. He lasted a record two meetings.

The truth is that many Christians are more RELIGIOUS than they are Christian and the same principles of attraction and repulsion apply, that is, unclean spirits of religiosity which have been passing themselves off as the HOLY Spirit are equally appalled at the REAL PRESENCE[2] of Christ as any other unclean spirit. These religious spirits love playing games and masquerading as the Holy spirit, parading their religiosity for the admiration of the undiscerning, but when the HOLY spirit is present in burning power to cleanse and deliver, it becomes all rather too dangerous even for them, and so both non-Christians and Christians who have an appearance and measure of Godliness may be discomforted and repelled by powerful, searching ministries that expose pollution; deep, hidden, inner pollution, without really knowing why in their conscious minds.

(v) RIGHT THING - WRONG TIME

It is usually right to praise the Lord and read the Scriptures; indeed the Word of God says we are to rejoice always and pray without ceasing (1 Thess. 5:16-17). But if you were reading the Word of God on a beach while someone was drowning a few feet away from you most people would say that the good Lord would expect you to be a doer of His Word in that situation, not just a reader. (cf. James 1:21-25).

---

2. Not to be confused with the Anglo-Catholic doctrine concerning the bread and the wine in Holy Communion.

Likewise if you stood up in one of our meetings and began praising the Lord loudly and continuously during my preaching neither I nor the Lord would be impressed.

Also if you only **prayed** in the first situation (above) without acting to save the drowning person, or if you prayed out loud when someone is preaching, most Christians would think that was a bit odd, but perhaps find it difficult to express in words.

Religious spirits are very good at doing apparently good things at the WRONG time, cutting across the real leading of the Holy Spirit, shutting off revelations of the Holy Spirit such as discernment, prophecy, rhemas of the Word of God etc. They try to reduce our ability to receive genuine leadings of the Holy Spirit and at the same time draw attention to themselves, robbing us of His real presence and robbing the Lord of the glory that belongs to Him alone.

(vi) BIBLE DISCUSSION - BEWARE FANTASY

It is difficult to have a factual no-nonsense Bible discussion with someone who is manifesting a religious spirit. Discussion tends to become swamped in lyrical and romantic notions of fantasy with the hidden intent that the REAL message of the Scriptures be smothered in religious, gooey sentimentalism and/or self-righteousness, effectively preventing the logos (written Word) becoming a rhema (living Word). **Exaggeration is another very real and common indicator.**

(vii) UNCONDITIONAL LOVE - MORE FANTASY

For example how many times have you heard a young, starry-eyed Christian who is really going forward in the faith talk about **"the unconditional love of God."** It is not something that led to their conversion but a message they heard afterwards which sounded so good, so appealing and comforting.

The problem is, I can't find it in the Bible - at least not the way it is understood by many who believe it.

It is true that **we love (Him) because He first loved us** (1 John 4:19) but to suggest that *"once saved is always saved"* (with its logical conclusion that our Christian walk and discipleship doesn't REALLY matter) is presumptuous to say the least. Disastrous would be a more accurate description. Most people don't really understand that:

FAITH/BELIEF	means	PUT YOUR TRUST IN (COMMITMENT TO)
REPENTANCE	means	A COMPLETE CHANGE OF MIND and DIRECTION in obedience to the Lord.

We know we have the FAITH that saves us when it flows into OBEDIENCE:

> *"He who BELIEVES in the Son has eternal life, He who does not OBEY the Son shall not see life, but the wrath of God rests upon him". (John 3:36).*

Please note the interwoven relationship between BELIEF and OBEDIENCE. You can't get it any clearer than that! I like **the Salvation Army** principle that states we are saved by **OBEDIENT** FAITH!

Not only does the notion of **"unconditional love"** comfort people who are going on strong in the Lord it also "comforts" those who are on the broad road to destruction (Matt. 7:13-

14). They don't need false comfort - they need the truth! (cf. 1 Cor. 6:9-10). It leads to **universalism** which attempts to deceive us with the notion that ALL roads lead to Almighty God, contradicting Jesus' words *"I am the Way... No one comes to the Father except through me!"*

Not only will you not find the notion of "unconditional love" in the Bible, except by interpreting verses such as 1 John 4:10, 19 (above) to mean far more than they really say, but there are a number of Scriptures that quite clearly tell us the opposite:

> " **.... He who loves me (Jesus)** shall be loved by my Father, and I will love Him ... (John 14:21).

> "**.... If anyone loves Me, he will keep my words**, and My Father will love him (John 14:24).

> "**....** the Father Himself loves you **BECAUSE you have loved Me and have believed...** (John 16:27).

> "**....** For this is the love of God **IN ORDER THAT we keep His commandments ...**" (1 John 5:3).

So the Word of God tells us that once the Lord has set His love upon us and brought us into the knowledge of Himself, He has certain expectations of us.

That is clear enough, isn't it? We are to:

- *love Jesus*
- *keep the words of Jesus*
- *believe (that Jesus came from the Father)*
- *keep God's commandments*

These ***conditions*** obtain for us the (continuing) love of God. (See also Neh. 1:5, 8-9, Isa. 45:9, Prov. 16:3, Matt. 7:21, 18:3; Luke 13:3, John 3:3, 6:53, 15:6-14 etc).

What of the notion of **"God's unconditional love"?** It is a typical religious deception. It is like a waterless cloud (cf. Jude 12). It sounds good but will destroy many whose faith tends to be built upon fantasy rather than sound and careful interpretations of God's Word.

(viii) MARRIED TO JESUS - MORE FANTASY

Another religious notion that you may hear uttered by a Christian sister is *"I'm married to Jesus"*. It is good to be devoted to Him, to be a true disciple or even an anointed minister, but as far as I know the Wedding of the Lamb has not come yet. If the Bridegroom has come and the Wedding has taken place, I am, of all disciples, most to be pitied, because **I MISSED OUT!!** - and so have a lot of other believers.

If you are part of the **Bride of Christ**, that fifty percent of the **Body of Christ** that makes up the Wise Maidens then it may be truthful to say you are **BETROTHED** to Him (2 Cor. 11:2), but MARRIED? I don't think so. One day, God willing, you will be going up into the clouds (1 Thess. 4:17), but for the moment please come down to earth!

3.2   SELF-MUTILATION–ANCESTRAL CHAINS

There is so much of this destructive activity of cutting one's own body with knives and razors going on today but, to my knowledge, no one has yet identified it as being inspired by a **religious spirit.**

The prophets and priests of BAAL did this as part of their religious rites (1 Kings 18:26-28). Likewise today, through-out the world primitive cultures that are based on a witch-craft religion continue to practice self-mutilation. Our own

Aboriginal people, those who are still locked into their tribal rites, allegedly continue this practice today.[3]

The problem is not unknown in our psychiatric hospitals indicating possible transference from primitive cultures to western cultures. This should not surprise us because for every indigenous person who becomes a Christian there are probably two westernised people who sink back into occultism (BAAL worship). In addition *ancestral (hereditary) pollution* can go back many generations.

However, what is becoming noticeable is that this condition is being linked with **Multiple Personality Disorder (M.P.D.),** more recently re-named **Dissociate Identity Disorder (D.I.D.).**[4]

Radio legend John Laws, on his morning **2UE Radio** talkback program (7 March '99) interviewed a **Cameron West** who had written a book about the many "personalities" that controlled his life and for which he blamed child sexual abuse. At least one of these personalities caused him to inflict blows and/or cuts to himself. I first came across this condition in 1969 when, as a young Anglican curate I listened to a shocked housewife recount her horror at finding her soldier husband standing in front of the bathroom mirror and bleeding from self-inflicted cuts from his razor.

This peculiar behaviour is well attested to in the Word of God. We have the father of all multiple personality cases in the man with **the Legion** (of demons) whom the Lord Jesus Christ delivered (by casting out all the invaders) and

---

3 " Man, Myth and Magic" p.180
4 I have to say I am not impressed with the new label D.I.D.. You can call a serious "mental" problem what you like and play with words forever but that doesn't help the sufferer. M.P.D. IS adequate and ACCURATE. See Book 4 **"We All Have Our Demons"** for a full discussion.

restored to his right mind. (Mark 5:1-20). While he was ill he repeatedly cut himself with stones, among other things (v.5), apparently because his ancestors had worshipped the false god **BAAL**, and their religious spirits had been passed down the blood line[5] to him.

He didn't know why he performed such stupid, self-destructive actions on himself but **religious control spirits** simply took over in their turn, with the rest of the Legion of spirits, and he couldn't help himself (Compulsive Self Mutilation Disorder ???).[6]

Why did the prophets of BAAL cut themselves? When their prayers to their false god were not answered (after a full morning's concerted effort) they offered BAAL a BLOOD sacrifice. Not the blood of bulls and goats. Not the blood of their children (this time - cf. 2 Chron. 28:3. Psa. 106:37-38 etc.), but their OWN blood! It was their "best" effort, but it still didn't work (1 Kings 18:20-40) because they were opposing the Lord God and His prophet Elijah.

There are several Old Testament references forbidding self mutilation (Lev. 19:28, 21;5, Deut. 14:1, Jer. 16:6 etc.) but it is the story of "Legion" which inspires us because we learn about M.P.D., self mutilation and the demons inspiring and controlling all such unclean activity. Most importantly we learn of God's solution to the evil slavery. Unclean control spirits CAN be removed, and replaced by **God's Control Spirit - the Holy Spirit!** (Eph. 5:18 etc.) - in Jesus' Name!

We no longer have to sacrifice birds, animals and children like the pagans did (and do). We no longer have to shed

---

5   The soul is in the blood - Lev. 17:11,14 lit. Heb.
6   My best choice for Self Mutilation would be I.B.S.D. (Idolatrous, Blood sacrifice disorder), blunt but true!

OUR blood to please or appease pagan gods which are no gods, in reality (1 Cor. 8:5). Even our indigenous Aboriginal people have a tradition of shedding their blood during some of their tribal dances. It is part of their culture that has to be crucified (Rom. 6:3-7) if they are to enter the blessings of Almighty God. The **Lord Jesus Christ has shed HIS blood** in order to give us TOTAL victory, recorded in a LEGAL COVENANT (the New Testament) over ALL OUR ENEMIES. The apostle Paul's letter to the Colossians tells us that through the Cross of Christ, God has:

(a)   *made us alive together with Christ*
(b)   *forgiven us all our trespasses*
(c)   *cancelled the written laws (of God) against us*
(d)   *dropped His charges against us*
(e)   *nailed them to the Cross*
(f)   *thereby stripped the powers of darkness of their weapons against us*
(g)   *therefore shamefully exposed our enemies, and*
(h)   *triumphed over them by the Cross of Christ (Col. 2:13-15).*

What a victory! **It is a legal, spiritual victory that can be ours IF:**

(i)   *we are or become true disciples (John 8:31-32)*
(ii)   *understand this legal victory (above)*
(iii)   *know or learn how to appropriate this victory into our lives*
(iv)   *live in the light of it*

It's time for us all to move into it.

CHAPTER 4

PHARISAISM

4.1 THEN AND NOW

I remember a joke Dr Billy Graham told an audience many years ago (1968?) regarding a new convert. The man was a bit of a misfit but experienced a wonderful conversion. For three months he went along to his local church and tried to fit in.

Nobody was interested. They didn't believe in evangelism or sudden conversions. They thought Billy was a salesman and were suspicious of any "fruit" from his ministry. The new man felt shut out and rejected. As he desperately prayed one night, he said *"Lord I've tried and tried. Sorry, but I can't seem to get into that church." "That's okay",* replied the Lord. *"I can't get in there either!"*

There is no doubt that some churches have organised the Holy Spirit right out of their system. The meetings, the activities, the forms continue but the Spirit of God has long since gone. The saddest part is no one has noticed!

Just how "religious" the historic Church has become, and continues to be is easily demonstrated from history. **John Hus** was a livewire early reformer of the Church who was ex-communicated and burnt at the stake on 6th July, 1415, a hundred years before **John Calvin** and **Martin Luther** set Europe alight with the **Reformation.** Less than 300 years later **John Wesley** and his preachers were thrown out of British churches and forced to preach in the fields. Just as well, for the church buildings could not have contained the huge crowds who wanted to hear them, and so sparked the Christian revival of England in the eighteenth century. In this twentieth century we have seen the traditional churches' inability to cope with the Pentecostal movement to the extent that Christians who spoke in tongues, prophesied, and ministered deliverance and healing were forced out of their churches and obliged to form their own assemblies under the broad banner of **Pentecostalism.**

Now we have a new surge forward in what has become known as the **Renewal Movement,** incorporating Christians from every historic church denomination who are prepared to move forward with the Holy Spirit wherever He leads, regardless of any earlier Church tradition.

Let us ask ourselves the question *"Why is it that, down through 2000 years of history, the Church denominations of the day ALWAYS RESIST a fresh move of the Holy Spirit (Acts 7:51)?"* One answer is obviously that they are not guided by the Holy Spirit. The next obvious question, *"**Then with what spirit are they controlled?"*, **you can answer for yourself.** It is interesting to note that most Christian denominations which have clung to their traditions and resisted the Renewal move of God's Spirit today are in decline, perhaps because they did not know the time of their visitation from above (cf. Luke 19:41-48).

4.2 THE LEAVEN OF THE PHARISEES

It is very significant that when Jesus was born of Mary, and thirty years later, when He revealed Himself to Israel and began His ministry, He was not manifested to the religious community, the scribes, Pharisees and Sadducees.

Logically we would think that He would come first to those who knew and taught the Word of God to the people of Israel, but as has been pointed out so often for our encouragement, He came amongst the common people, and from the rawest members of society He chose His recruits, His disciples. Why?

I think one reason was that these rough and ready twelve disciples did not have to UN-LEARN all the religious training that a Pharisee would have had to un-learn. When **Saul** the Pharisee was converted on the road to Damascus while on a mission of persecution, he then had to spend three years in Arabia and Damascus, and a further fourteen years in Syria and Cilicia, sorting himself out before appearing before the Christian leaders in Jerusalem (Gal. 1:15-2:2). That is a total of *seventeen years* Saul (now **Paul**) needed to sort out his theology to the point where he was positioned to correct the apostle **Peter** and other Christian leaders of repute (Gal. 2:6-14).

So you can understand it is much harder for a Pharisee (who "knows" a lot) than it is for a fisherman, to receive revelation from Christ.

What was the hidden problem of the Pharisees? What did Jesus mean when He said for we disciples to beware the LEAVEN of the Pharisees, Sadducees and Herod? (Matt. 16:5-12, Mark 8:15).

In Hebrew life leaven came to play an important part, not only in bread-making, but also in law, ritual, and religious teaching. It was made originally from fine white bran kneaded with must; from the meal of certain plants such as fitch or vetch; or from barley mixed with water and then allowed to stand till it turned sour. As baking developed, leaven was produced from bread flour kneaded without salt and kept till it passed into a state of fermentation.

a) In bread – making

In bread–making the leaven was probably a piece of dough, retained from a former baking, which had fermented and turned acid. This was then either dissolved in water in the kneading–trough before the flour was added, or was 'hid' in the flour and kneaded along with it. The bread thus made was known as 'leavened', as distinct from 'unleavened' bread (Exod. 12:15, etc.). There is no clear trace of the use of other sorts of leaven, although it has often been suggested that the Jews used also the lees of wine as yeast.

b) In law and ritual

The earliest Mosaic legislation (Exod. 23:18,34:25) prohibited the use of leaven during the Passover and the 'feast of unleavened bread' (Exod. 23:15; Matt. 26:17, etc.). This was to remind the Israelites of their hurried departure from Egypt, when without waiting to bake leavened bread they carried dough and kneading – troughs with them, baking as they wandered (Exod. 12:24 ff.; Deut. 16:3, etc.), much as the Bedouin still do.

The prohibition on leaven (Lev. 2:11) was possibly made because fermentation implied disintegration and corruption, and to the Hebrew anything in a decayed state suggested uncleanness. Rabbinical writers often used leaven as a symbol of evil and of man's hereditary corruption, corrupting the mass of dough with which it is mixed.

Doubtless for this reason it was excluded also from the offerings placed upon the altar of the LORD, only cakes made from flour without leaven (Lev.10:12) being allowed.

c) In religious teaching

The figurative uses of leaven in the New Testament to a large extent reflect the former view of it as 'corrupt and corrupting'. Jesus utters warnings against the leaven of the Pharisees, Sadducees, and Herodians[1] (Matt.16:6; Mark 8:15)

So we can conclude that just as leaven spreads and permeates throughout the body of bread, so the religious traditions of men permeate throughout and sours (corrupts) every area of our attempts to worship God in spirit and in truth, if we don't watch out!

Just as an example, we know leaven often represents sin in the Bible (1Cor.5:6f, Gal.5:7-9) but even if we acknowledge bread is but a symbol of the Body of Christ in Holy Communion, why do some use bread with leaven in it to represent Christ's Body?

If we believe that our Lord Jesus was without the heart disease of original sin would it not be more honouring and appropriate to use Unleavened bread?– That is, bread without YEAST, which is readily available in the markets?

4.3 THE FEAR OF MAN (i.e. Man's Disapproval and Rejection)

The fear of men locks ministers into the traditions of men. Proverbs tells us that *"The fear of man brings a snare, but whoever puts his trust in the Lord shall be safe"*, and most ministers believe and teach this to their flocks. They delight to show the party unity of the Pharisees against

---

1   We acknowledge the contribution to the above historical information by Dr. J.D. Douglas of "Christianity Today", in the New Bible Dictionary (I.V.F.).

Jesus and rightly expose the misplaced loyalty of the Pharisees to each other when they should have been seeking
the truth.

Many ministers do not realise that they themselves have
been compromised by their peers and are consciously or
subconsciously influenced by the desire for esteem and
acceptance from their brother ministers. This clash of loyalties is always exposed when one's traditional peer grouping is upset by a fresh reforming work of the Holy Spirit,
hence Stephen could say to the Jews before they stoned
him *"you **always** resist the Holy Spirit!"* It is not that anyone
wants to be wrong or deceived. It is just that without our
realising it, the enemy has often worked us into a position
where we have been conditionally compromised in our loyalties, and peer group pressure becomes the greatest single
shaping factor in our ministries, even more than the Lord.
To make matters worse we hate anyone to even suggest
this is so. Stephen's comments to his critics in full were:

> *"You stiff-necked people, UNCIRCUMCISED in
> HEART and EARS, you always resist the Holy
> Spirit. As your fathers did, so do you." (Acts
> 7:51).*

When I was being prepared for Ordination the Diocese required me to go on an Ordinands Retreat, where, with
eleven other young men, we prayed and meditated before
taking the final plunge into the Ministry. I was the only charismatic in the group (back in 1967) and most of the others
kept out of my way. However, one afternoon we went off in
different directions for individual walks and I found myself
joined by an earnest young man who began to ask me many
questions about my experience of the Holy Spirit. Suddenly
a couple of other ordinands appeared in view, and equally
suddenly my companion began to walk very quickly. Be-

cause I was speaking earnestly at the time, I kept pace with
him at first, without thinking, but then I realised as he
speeded up even more, that he was trying to put distance
between us so that he would not be seen talking to me and
have his "conservative evangelical" reputation tarnished. It
was a real "Nicodemus" situation. He wanted and sought
the truth but not at the expense of the suspicions of his peers
or to put in jeopardy his acceptance by them.

The apostle John put it rather bluntly when he said that the
Pharisees *"loved the praise (glory) of men more than the
praise (glory) of God"* (John 12:43), while Jesus asked them
*"How can you believe (the truth) when you receive glory
from each other, and do not seek glory from the only God*
(John 5:44). Paul says that a man is a true Jew who is one
INWARDLY and true CIRCUMCISION is of the heart, spiri-
tual not literal. *"His praise is not from men but from God."*
(Rom 2:29)

So the scripture warns us in several places that fear of man
and the seeking of acceptance, recognition, praise and self-
glory from man locks us into our traditions by hiding the truth
from us and gets us no praise from the Lord. Let us resolve to
get the priorities of our respective loyalties right with the Lord
and be finished with compromised or polluted loyalties forever, which reflect an uncircumcised heart and ears.

4.4 PHARISAIC TRADITION

Pharisees took their name from a Hebrew word which
signifies division or separation because they distinguished
themselves from the other Israelites by a more strict manner
of life which they professed. They developed human
traditions in addition to God's Word and sought to make a
great show of religion in outward things. They were proud,
covetous, unjust, superstitious and hypocritical. When our

Saviour appeared in Judea the Pharisees held great sway among the people because of the legend they had built up of their great learning, sanctity of life-style and exact observance of the Law. They often fasted, made long prayers, paid tithes scrupulously and distributed alms, but all this was corrupted by a spirit of proud ostentation, hypocrisy and self-love. They wore fringes and borders at the corners and hems of their garments broader than the other Jews as a badge of distinction and as greater observers of the Law than others. In matters of religion the traditions of the patriarchs were the chief subject of their studies and to these they made additions of their own as they thought fit. By this means they had overburdened the Law of God with a vast number of trifling observances that were useless and which made a heavy and impossible yoke upon the necks of the Hebrew people. They even altered and corrupted parts of the Law according to their own interpretations as our Saviour Himself reproached them. For example, the Law commands us to honour our father and mother, however the Pharisees taught that if we say to our parents that are in necessity "Father or mother, the need you ask of me is dedicated to God" we were then freed from the obligation of helping our parents.

The observance of the Sabbath was another point about which the Lord often corrected them. They found fault with people who brought their sick to be healed, they were scandalised that a man carried away his bed on the Sabbath day after he had been cured of paralysis, from which they concluded that our Lord could not be a man sent from God because he failed to observe that Day of rest, in their eyes.

The Lord upbraided them for making long prayers while standing up in the synagogues or at the corners of the streets, and in pretence of long prayers consume widows' houses. He also reproached them for travelling sea and land to make a proselyte (convert) and after that make him an even greater sinner than he was before by teaching him falsely and making him even more opposed to the Gospel, instead of embracing it. Jesus said they affect to build up the tombs of the old prophets and to openly declare they disapproved of the actions of their forefathers who persecuted the prophets of old, while they themselves were **motivated by the same spirit** and opposed all those who brought God's correction to them. Please refer to Appendix C for all the relevant scriptures.

It is the easiest thing in the world for Christians to see the leaven (spiritual disease) of the Pharisees (Luke 12:1) in other Christians, and sometimes very hard to see it in ourselves. I remember being very impressed with a young clergyman **(Rev. David West)** many years ago when he said *"There is a measure of the Pharisee in all of us (clergymen)!"* I was impressed because previously I seemed to be the only one who thought that way. To be fair, I think a lot of ministers have probably perceived it, but it is not something which is thought of as helpful or profitable to emphasise. Most of us simply try to see it in ourselves and quietly train ourselves to overcome it, which is not so easy because it can be so subtle (snaky). It is much easier to see the splinter in our brother's eye than to see the beam in our own eye (Matt. 7:3-5).

It should be understood that David West was speaking to me (above) about ourselves and our friends serving in the Anglican Diocese of Sydney. Most of us belong(ed) to the **Conservative Evangelical** tradition with its strong emphasis on the biblical teachings of the Protestant Reformation. During our training days at **Moore Theological College** the Vice Principal[1] shocked a class of students I was in by saying:

---

1   The Rev. Canon **Donald Robinson** went on to become the ninth Archbishop of Sydney, retiring in 1993.

"The Pharisees were the conservative evangelicals of their day"

That was a brave thing for a conservative evangelical to say, but it is true. I still remember the audible gasp of horror that came from some of the students. Hopefully it was a lesson we have never forgotten.

Probably the greatest flaw in the Pharisees make-up, the real leaven that so polluted them was that **they loved the praise of men,** the praise of their cronies (friends, mates) whom they would have known since they trained for the priesthood at the (theological) college of Hillel back in their youth, **more than the praise of God!** (John 5:44, 12:42-43, cf. Mark 8:38, Matt. 10:28, Acts 7:51-53, Rom. 2:29, Gal. 1:10, I Thess. 2:4, Prov. 29:25).

And isn't that what most Christian ministers do? We almost all have fond memories of our student days - of fellow students who struggled to study alongside us - of lecturers whose diligence, learning and knowledge we were compelled to respect, to the point where they were considered to be right on just about everything we studied.

All this adds up to a clash of loyalties when the Holy Spirit brings us **a revelation from an outsider!** Unfortunately **long term loyalties** and **soulish links** almost always ensure that we *"do always resist the Holy Spirit!"* (Acts 7:51). These **religious chains**, forged over many years, are the hardest to break. Thank God He breaks them!

Do you remember the warnings of the Word of God that we shared with you earlier?

"Beware in case there is anyone robbing (making a victim of) you through *philosophy* and *empty deceit:*

(i) ***according to the tradition of men***

(ii) ***according to the elemental spirits of the world and not according to Christ!" (Col. 2:8).***

*"If you died (with Christ) from the **elemental spirits of the world**, why do you live in the world as if you were subject to its decrees (human philosophy and tradition)? (Col. 2:20).*

That is a good question, isn't it?

These **religious chains, traditions** created and forged by men who were under the inspiration of **religious spirits**, the **elemental spirits** (stoicheia),[2] are the hardest to break.

Thank God that, with Him, all things are possible.

4.5   DEFINITION OF "RELIGIOUS SPIRIT"

I think it is now time to attempt a definition of "religious spirit".

This may not be the greatest definition in the world, but to my knowledge no one has ever defined or described the function of an unclean religious spirit before, so here goes:

A religious spirit is an unclean spirit seeking to achieve one or more of the following:

---

2 The word **"stoicheia"** (elements) seems something of a mystery to the translators of the New Testament. The **International Critical Commentary** on the Epistle to the **Galatians** by **Ernest D. Burton** discusses **"stoicheia"** for nine scholarly pages. Cutting through all the intellectual waffle and consideration of the evidence one sentence stands out:
"This evidence ... leaves no doubt that stoicheion (singular) did eventually come to mean an ***"angel", "spirit",*** or ***"god"*** (p.513).
This confirms the translation of the Revised Standard Version (and others?) of **"elemental spirits"**.

(a) **Replace the effective worship of The Creator** (Almighty God, through the Lord Jesus Christ) throughout the Creation, with the worship of the demonic gods of this world by means of idolatry and alternative religions.

(b) Hinder, pull down, replace, mock and destroy the genuine, spiritual worship and communion of Christians with their Lord.

(c) **Parade its own religiosity** with a view to:

   (i)   advertising its "spirituality" (holier than thou!)[3]
   (ii) establishing a spiritual "superiority" over "lesser" Christians.
   (iii) establishing its own false "righteousness"

(d) **Express religious lies, deception and/or fantasy.**

This includes *spiritualising* the natural, for example, seeing God's *supernatural* power at work when He has used his *natural* power (nature – e.g. rain) to answer prayer.

Rain may be answered prayer, but it is not a miracle. A miracle is the manifestation of a remarkable or marvellous event, *usually contrary to nature!*

I offer this definition as a combination of the Word of God and experience in the deliverance ministry.

---

3   See Isaiah 65:2-5 (Note v5)-Authorised (K.J.) or Revised Version.

CHAPTER 5

DANGERS IN RENEWAL

5.1   RELIGIOUS EXHIBITIONISM

Attending a medium-sized charismatic church in Sydney I was amazed to find myself seated behind a lady who, during each worship song, arose and performed a wriggly dance in the style of a Baghdad belly dancer. There may be a place for holy dancing in worship, based on the precedent set by **King David** (2 Sam. 6:14). I'm not into it myself and the jury is still out on the matter, as far as I'm concerned, but we would not want to make the mistake of **Michal**, David's wife. However, the incident above was blatant exhibitionism.

The wriggly arms and body movements were so snaky it did not surprise me when the Pastor commented *"Sometimes I worry about you, sister"*. Neither did it surprise when she signalled to go on stage so she could share a vision she had just been given. It was some religious, useless thing I can't even remember today, about as valuable as a fifty cent watch. No wonder the apostle Paul warned us NOT to take our stand on visions (Col. 2:18).

Later in the program I was invited to say a few words as a visiting minister, and could not resist warning the assembly about religious behaviour inspired by deceiving spirits. My comments were well received but there are no prizes for guessing which person was nodding most vigorously in agreement!!

She just couldn't keep out of the action!

Some time ago I wrote the following in one of our **Full Salvation Fellowship** Newsletters:

"Some churches prefer to run a drama (creative arts) program rather than a deliverance (cleansing) program. I wonder why?"

I have always had a wariness towards Church Creative Arts programs and schools because it is so obviously an area in our lives in which it is so easy to fulfil **the lusts of the flesh, the lust of the eyes and the pride of life** (1 John 2:16).

And even if ALL comes under the control of the Holy Spirit (and that can be a big **IF!**), we then have to challenge its level of PRIORITY in a church or ministry. There are questions that need to be asked:

1. How much TIME does it take out of the pastoral week?

2. What is the price tag for all the tuition and equipment?

3. What scriptural support is there for any particular art?

4. (How) Is it bearing fruit for the Kingdom of God?

These are not necessarily NEGATIVE questions designed to pour cold water on ALL art skills.

For example question 3 can produce much scriptural support for musicians - no problem, and there is some support for dancing, but I have always been concerned it is so easy for a stage presentation to degenerate into entertainment for the audience on earth, rather than worship for the Audience on the Throne in Heaven.

However I must add that although the lusts of the flesh etc. are an ever present danger in many types of ministry (e.g. *preaching to impress PEOPLE with self* rather than presenting the Christ) the few segments of worship dancing I have seen have been beautifully done unto the Lord!

Question 4 presents us with the bottom line and the acid test. Is the Lord, the everlasting and almighty God magnified and glorified through an activity, and the Kingdom of God extended? (cf. Matt. 12:28). The good news is that MANY people have (to my limited knowledge) been saved through dramatic presentations of the sinful, hopeless state of mankind and the grace of God in providing a Saviour, Who is Christ the Lord!

Perhaps we could add to the old saying "It's not what you do but the **way** that you do it", the words "... and the reason **WHY** you do it!" The final question to be answered is:

5.   What are our MOTIVES?

5.2 COUNTERFEIT GIFTS

Lying and religious spirits may bring forth a false prophetic Word if they feel it will give them the pre-eminence in the Assembly, and there is no one sufficiently experienced present to detect them. Such "prophecies" are not always doctrinally inaccurate but may be simply insipid - having no real message or value at all.

For example, some prophets will continuously tell you *"Thus says the Lord, I love you ..."* There may be times when you need to hear that, but you know it from the Holy Spirit in you, and you can read it in the Word, so you don't really need a prophet to tell you that God loves you almost every meeting.

Another very common revelation is that God has got big plans for you. If you will just make a couple of minor adjustments to your life then God will mightily use you and make you into a great vessel of honour.

* **You are going to be rich!**

* **You are going to be great!**

Praise the Lord!

Such revelations rarely happen, but by the time the "guidance" has fallen apart nobody else remembers it anyway (if it is not recorded) and it is conveniently buried in the past.

During the **Reformation** of the sixteenth century the Born Again Church of England had Formularies and Articles of Religion drawn up which includes a sermon encouraging the right use of the gifts of the Holy Spirit (Article 35, Homily 16) but the Church quickly fell back into ritual prayer book stuff.

This meant that prophets, both true and false, had to become independent and form their own groups. After healthy beginnings these groups were (and are) often infiltrated by the subtle deceptions of the devil and become sects. Even genuine stigmatics have been known to greatly err in this way.

A distressed mother rang me recently to say how her beautiful Spirit-filled son, who was on fire for the Lord, came under the influence of an independent prophetess and in a short space of time claimed to be a prophet himself. He now accuses his mother (also a committed Renewal Christian) and sister of harlotry and practicing witchcraft. A sweet, gentle young man has become a screaming accuser. Beware of lady prophets, evangelists, healers and stigmatics[1] who take control of a whole group, fellowship or a church. This is contrary to the Word of God. Ladies who **exercise** authority but are not themselves **under** authority (1 Cor. 11:3,16) are vulnerable to the powers of darkness, neither can they protect men from them.[2]

Again it is the FRUIT of the Spirit which identifies a true servant of the Lord, NOT the gifting of signs, wonders, prophecies etc. (Matt. 7:15-23).

I think that today, although it is not always easy, prophets and especially lady prophetesses who are usually more spiritually sensitive than men, need to find a Pastor and a church to which they are submitted. They need their prophecies recorded, transcribed, weighed by others and filed for future cosideration of fulfilment and accuracy.

A submitted and weighed prophet (1 Cor. 14:29) is usually much more trustworthy than an independent prophet, although there may be times they have to bring forth a "hard" word of correction (appeal, entreaty – 1 Cor. 14:3).

(i)   CLAIRVOYANCE

A classic example of a counterfeit gift seeking to mislead and obstruct a Christian ministry is presented to us in the Acts of the Apostles. **Paul** is preaching the gospel of Jesus to **Macedonians** in the city of **Philippi.**

> *"As we went to the place of prayer a certain maid with **a spirit of a python** met us, who brought much gain to her masters by practising soothsaying*

---

1   Verlie is also stigmatic – see **"Christian Authority and Power and the Stigmata",** chapter 3.
2   See **"Headcovering and Lady Pastor-Teachers",** chapter 5.

(divination). [17] She followed after Paul and us, crying out **'These men are bond slaves of the Most High God, who proclaim to you the way of salvation'.** *[18] And this she did over many days. But Paul became greatly troubled and turned to the spirit and said, 'I* **charge you in the Name of Jesus Christ to come out from her'.** *And it came out the same hour". (Acts 16:16-18).*

Clearly the enemy has counterfeit gifts to at least match the nine gifts of the Holy Spirit listed in 1 Cor. 12:7-10, and they are not always easy to discern. Even the apostle Paul had to wait many days before getting the discernment he needed. After all, the girl was telling the truth in describing Paul and Silas as bond-servants to God who preached the way of salvation.

This is what confounds so many Christians today, as it nearly did Paul. Religious spirits can and will present a good deal of truth in order to achieve their unclean mission, but of course, this **python spirit** was a classic example of the enemy saying **the right thing at the wrong time**. It is equivalent to a member of your church standing up and reading the Word of God out loud while your Pastor is trying to preach a message. The result would be disastrous. She (it) must have driven Paul nearly out of his mind with her constant harassment and interruptions. He needed a few days to check things with the Lord, and then - **POW!** The snaky deception was over!

Christians who have genuine gifts of the Holy Spirit, such as prophecy, should know there can be occasions when an unclean spirit will seek to break in and take over the message, or whatever is happening. The activity of religious spirits infiltrating other genuine vocal gifts such as tongues[1] and prophecy is a very subtle attack upon the Holy Spirit inspired proclamation of the pure Word of God and is designed to nullify the power of the Word, and to confuse and mislead. "But" you say, "Surely the Lord would not allow that?" Well, the truth is that it happens all the time (1 Tim. 4:1-3), because Christians generally are so unaware of the kind of spirit with which they speak. But, praise the Lord, He is giving the Renewal Church more and more perception with which to discern the truth.

It is not that the speakers are aware of their spirit so much as the hearers. The speakers are usually quite sincere and genuine but are themselves deceived. They usually give words of knowledge or describe vision upon vision in technicolour which never seem to come to fruition. Prophecies inspired **totally by religious spirits** seem to be less common, perhaps because *it is easier to remain undetected from the weighing of other prophets if the misguidance can be threaded into a genuine prophecy.* This "mixture" may then achieve the result of bringing a genuine Word into disrepute, because of a measure of distortion, so it is rendered ineffective or even destructive.

(ii)   EXAMINE YOURSELF!

Genuinely gifted vessels should be careful to tune into the Lord and check the spirit/Spirit before they actually speak. I remember an Anglican Renewal Conference held in Port Macquarie in 1992, with Bishops, Clergy and lay people present in which the Lord "forced" me to prophesy, after six promptings by the Spirit. Towards the end of the prophecy

---

1   We acknowledge here the existence of false or demonic tongues, of course. Test the spirits.

the Lord told the assembly (through me) to *"come before Me in repentance and renewal..."*

I balked at telling this mature gathering to repent. I remember a shock-wave hitting my spirit, and in that thousandth of a second I asked *"Surely you don't want me to tell **these people** to repent Lord? That can't be right, can it? They repented when they became Christians and then they experienced major repentance again when they came into renewal. Do you really want me to tell them to repent some more?" "Yes", said the Lord, "Tell them again to repent!"* So I did (speaking for the Lord) and so did **Bishop Hamish** of **Bunbury Diocese** when he preached that evening, confirming the prophetic word.

What I hedged about saying in a few seconds, the Bishop hammered for more than an hour! The Lord really wanted to get His point across then, and the point I am making now is that we all will experience the enemy seeking to break into genuine gifts and pollute them, either totally or in part, and there needs to be a constant checking (weighing, judging - 1 Cor. 14:29) moment to moment, during the operation of ANY gift or leading which requires us to act.

Experienced preachers who want to preach Jesus but fall into the snare of preaching or teaching intellectualism are a classic example. The pride in them overrules their spirit and the Holy Spirit has no free course in their hearts. They unconsciously preach to impress men with SELF and not to lift up Jesus, so they give their flocks dry stones instead of living bread. It's so very easy to do - I know - and such religiosity is not of the Lord.

A clergyman friend of mine (yes, I still have a few!) resigned from his denomination and I asked him why he had done so. He had not been viewed with anything like the suspicion

I had been subjected to since moving into Deliverance ministry. He was in Renewal with an emphasis on prayer and intercession, drawing closer to God, so why did he resign?

"The Church (organisation) is controlled by a religious spirit", he told me simply.

Even though I have not resigned from my own denominational Orders and links, and am still an accredited minister of the Anglican Church of Australia (although not under a Bishop's oversight), I could not disagree with him.

CHAPTER 6

OUTSIDE THE CHURCHES

6.1 IN THE HOME

I suppose the most obvious example of the activity of a religious spirit in the home is demonstrated when a Christian spouse seeks to bring his or her un-saved spouse into the knowledge of the Lord.

Let us assume for the purpose of illustration it is the wife that is converted and the husband is resisting the invitation of the Lord. The root cause may be that the husband's soul is in a mess and when the Holy Spirit comes into the wife's soul, all the sin and uncleanness in the husband's soul takes fright, knowing that the one-flesh situation means an unbelieving spouse is sanctified by the believing spouse (1 Cor. 7:14) and therefore **every unclean kingdom in his heart is threatened by the arrival of the Holy Spirit into his wife's heart.**

However, on many occasions the root cause of continuing division between the man and wife after her conversion is that not only does the wife have the HOLY Spirit but she also has religious spirits in her soul which raise their ugly heads at every opportunity.

Husbands of Godly women with a mixture of religious spirits in their soul can receive a very hard time. If it was truly the Holy Spirit speaking to them consistently, through their wives, many, many more of them would be converted, because there is such a fresh, cleansing, uplifting, liberating beauty with the Spirit of Christ. But if the wife "comes on strong" with a "pious", sickly, revolting, suffocating, super-spiritual act with all its religious, legalistic criticism and self-righteous rules and regulations, and constantly removes herself from under her husband's headship by prefacing everything SHE wants with **"The Lord said",** thus effectively reducing her husband's considerations to ZERO in value, it is no wonder that he digs his toes in and rejects such an unclean lordship over his life. He doesn't know why and he can't put it into words, but he is just not going to submit to that kind of domination, and who can blame him? Deep within himself he thinks if that kind of syrupy religiosity is the hallmark or characteristic of Christianity he is better off as he is. Thanks, but no thanks!

The good news is that it is not, in this case, the Lord he is rejecting but a religious spirit. When someone gets around to showing him the truth of the beauty of Jesus, unclouded by the uncleanness he sees in Jesus' disciples (followers) THEN he has every chance of being born again by the will of God (John 1:13). In the meantime however, the sad consequence is that in rejecting the unclean religious domination of his wife he also blocks himself off from the Lord Jesus - the Saviour he needs so much! It hardly needs to be added that this husband and wife situation can be reversed with the husband having the self-righteous problem.

Dear Christian spouse - What can you do?

Well, the first thing to do (by the wife in this illustration) is to turn to the Scriptures for wisdom, and do what it says:

> "Wives, be in subjection to your own husbands so that even if any do not obey the Word, **they will be gained by the behaviour of their wives,** without the Word, observing your reverent and pure behaviour.
>
> (1 Peter 3:1-2)

So the key to a wife's (spouse's) campaign to win the heart of an unbelieving spouse for Christ Jesus in NOT to try to badger or control THEM but (first of all) control YOURSELF!! They may still fail but, if they do, you will not be at all to blame.

> *Do not let your outward appearance be of the World, with plaiting of hair and putting on ornaments of gold and clothing of (wealthy or fashion) garments but (rather be clothed with) the hidden man of the heart (Jesus) with **the incorruptibility of the meek and quiet (human) spirit** which is of great value before God". (1 Peter 3:1-4, literal translation with bracketed words inserted by me).*

Obviously **it is not the Word alone[1] but the Spirit which is important in communicating God's truth to unbelieving spouses.** And not only is it what we say but the WAY we say it, i.e. **the spirit by which you say it** that is important. Especially our own conduct says more than a thousand words.

Cut out the religiosity. Cut out "The Lord said ..." attitude, He probably didn't say it at all and you are promoting a lie that has deceived YOU! Test the spirits. Examine the results you are getting from your guidance. Every time you say "The Lord said ..." record it in a book (with the date) and watch for its fruit. Remember that in the vast majority of cases the voice of the Lord is a still small voice and the

---

1   There are two Greek words translated WORD in English: (i) **Logos**, which means a legal, positional, covenantal word and (ii) **rhema** which means a LIVING, experiential word which is alive and applies NOW! It is the Holy Spirit that makes the LEGAL word alive for us and turns the **Logos** into a **Rhema** or, alternatively, brings a prophecy or a word of knowledge compatible with the **Logos** word.

message He gives you in your spirit is usually confirmed by two or three witnesses independently of yourself. That is, get confirmation from the Lord before you start putting His Name to your ideas which involve other people, at least until you have had proven success in **knowing** the leading of the Spirit.

He will confirm His guidance to you from totally unexpected sources - one of them may even be your husband or wife, if you care to listen ... Even then, train yourself to take responsibility for what you say, e.g. **"I believe** the Lord is saying ..."

6.2   IN THE PSYCHIATRIC WARD

There are a fairly high percentage of people suffering from mental disorders and receiving psychiatric counselling who ritualistically go through questionable religious activities - some may be genuinely Christian activities - others certainly are not. The psychiatrist can be faced with any one of the following situations:

(i)   **The genuine Christian** who not only has the Holy Spirit and wants to exercise valid Christian worship, but nevertheless has **other demonic or physical problems** for which the psychiatrist would seem to be God's answer to their needs. In this case genuine Christian activity can be mistaken for a "religious problem."

Back in 1975(?) I remember one young lady who was obviously a born-again Christian but who had a dramatic background of lack of care and broken relationships. She was one of those people who you would think of as a victim, a prey rather than a predator. She loved the Lord but lacked stability in her early life.

One day I received a 'phone call from her asking me to visit her in a psychiatric hospital. When I arrived she was in tears. Apparently she had been badgering the psychiatrists to let her go, saying she was fine and that Jesus would heal her if she needed any healing.

The more she claimed divine help the more the hospital staff thought she needed THEM! What really convinced them she should be kept in hospital were the regular tears, the praying out loud in the Ward, even to the point where she would drop to her knees in the middle of the Ward and cry out to the Lord to get her out of there!

Cries of desperation perhaps, but not wise! She was not all right. She was saying the right words but her behaviour was decidedly bizarre and unstable, and there was no way she was going to get out until her behaviour became "normal," according to the doctors.

I think this was my first experience of closely perceiving the dilemma of the medical profession. *No wonder so many of those involved in psychiatric work believe that religion, any religion, is a problem that needs curing.*

Even I could not always discern when the Holy Spirit or when the religious spirit was operating, so what hope would a psychiatrist - even a Christian psychiatrist - have? We are totally dependent upon discernment from the Lord in this!

(ii) **The genuine Christian** who is overtaken by unclean religious spirits and exercises *worship in a way that is hypocritical, fleshly, counterfeit and "showy"*, and brings the Christian faith into grave disrepute. *Religious display for the purpose of getting attention* is repulsive to Christian and non-

Christian observers alike and is often responsible for the charge "hypocrites" being unfairly levelled at all church-going Christians.

(iii) The non-Christian who has not been born again and who has the same problems as (ii) and practices a mockery of Christian worship. There is no redeeming quality here whatsoever and the true faith is again brought into disrepute. There is no Holy Spirit present, only the unclean counterfeit.

(iv) The non-Christian religious practitioner who wants to exercise the faith of his choice and thus draws strength from the demonic powers which (unbeknown to him) made him sick in the first place and therefore can never be substantially helped, e.g. a transcendental meditation advocate who hallucinates during or after meditation.

CONCLUSION

From the non-Christian psychiatrist's point of view it would appear that the patient's religion is a major factor contributing to their mental illness and therefore the less religious activity the better. While this may be true in some cases, it is unfortunate that a genuine work of God's grace tends to be confused with or viewed as something from which the patient should be cured. Unless the psychiatrist is an informed Christian he or she is most unlikely to be able to make the necessary distinctions, which are spiritually discerned.

CHAPTER 7

COUNTERFEITS OF THE NAME
ABOVE EVERY NAME!

Every Christian SHOULD know the importance, value and potential power available with the right use of the wonderful Name of the Lord JESUS Christ, for the Word of God makes clear that:

> *"... God has highly exalted Him and given Him the Name above EVERY name, that at the name of JESUS EVERY knee of heavenly beings and earthly beings and beings under the earth should bow, and every tongue confess that Jesus Christ is LORD, to the glory of God the Father!"*
>
> (Phil. 2:9-11).

> *"... And there is no salvation in anyone else for there is no other Name under Heaven given among men by which it is necessary for us to be saved".*
>
> (Acts 4:12).

7.1 THE FALSE JESUS SPIRIT

One of the more difficult things to do in discerning of spirits is distinguishing between the false or counterfeit Jesus spirit and the real Spirit of Christ. The apostle Paul links preaching a false Jesus with a false or different spirit and a different gospel (2 Cor. 11:4).

In my early days as a curate and in the Holy Spirit Renewal movement an Emu Plains housewife was converted by the

Lord, but during my follow-up visits I began to feel troubled in spirit. This lady was always saying *"The Lord told me to ...."* *"Jesus said to ......".*

I had been a Christian for nine (9) years and the Lord had only spoken audibly to me twice in all that time!

When people do this, what can you say? They have effectively "pulled rank" on you because **IF** the Lord has spoken it is time for everyone else to shut up.

In the very act of someone promoting their spirituality by claiming to get loud and clear direct guidance from the Throne of God, in reality they effectively cut themselves off from the wisdom of God's ministers. They are not open to a different view and can become impossible to pastor.

What is left but to speak the truth in love (Eph. 4:15) and pray the good Lord will give them the grace to examine their guidance.

I didn't know what to make of it then, and it is still a problem needing discernment today. Looking back, I suspect she was a closet (undiagnosed) schizophrenic and an unclean control spirit was desperately trying to undo her conversion to Christ; perhaps seed on stony ground (Mark 4:5-6).

It is a fairly common occurrence today for people who hear voices in their head to be told by a voice to attack people, commit crimes and even murder. These voices sometimes identify themselves as Jesus. The following media report is an example:

> *"The Manly (Sydney) Court was told that one of the women was attacked as she walked along Tower Street, Manly. She was punched in the mouth, knocked to the ground and had her handbag stolen.*

A second woman was also punched and knocked to the ground in Raglan Street, Manly.

A young man is alleged to have signed statements admitting all offences, having told police he acted in such a way "because Jesus wanted him to seek retribution from the bad ladies of Manly".

In one instance he had punched one woman in the face, knocked her to the ground, kicked her in the lower back and said: "Jesus wants this".[1]

7.2   THE NAME JESUS - ITS USE, MISUSE AND ABUSE

The famous English bard **William Shakespeare** unintentionally misled us when he wrote:

"What's in a name? That which we call a rose by any other name would smell as sweet". (Romeo and Juliet)

Shakespeare was speaking of names for IDENTIFICATION only.

It is true the names men entitle or call anything may be pure romanticism and quite uninformative as regards the character or substance of any particular object. However in the Bible names have specific MEANINGS which reveal the nature of the thing named as well as identify the personality.

---

1   Manly Daily, Jan. 15, 1988.

For example, prophecies of the Lord Jesus Christ's first coming say:

> *"His Name shall be called Wonderful Counsellor, Mighty God, Everlasting Father, Prince of Peace"*   *(Isaiah 9:6)*

> *"….. you shall call His Name Jesus, for He will save His people from their sins."*   *(Matt. 1:21)*

We also know from a literal translation of John chapter 17 that the Father has given Jesus His own (the Father's) Name, just as men today pass on their own names to their children.

> *"Holy Father,[2] keep them in your Name,* **which (Name) you have given to me …** *(v.11).*

> *"While I was with them I kept them in your Name,* **which you have given me….** *(v.12).*
> *"I have made known to them your Name…."* *(v.26).*

The name Jesus actually comes from two Hebrew words, **JAH** and **Hosea,** which means combined, **JAH (God) (is) Saviour.**

So you can see that the Name of Jesus is not just for identification only but carries the most powerful message for the human race!

What do you make of the Name of Jesus? The full identification is **"Lord Jesus Christ"** and there is no mistaking the identity of the One you are addressing when

---

2   It is not a good idea to call the Pope "Holy Father".

you use the three-fold titles and Name. **"Jesus Christ of Nazareth"** is also an accurate identification. Although there may have been others named Jesus over the centuries who came from Nazareth, there is only one Jesus of Nazareth who is *the Christ!*

In the English speaking nations almost no-one names their son Jesus but in some Latin/Spanish speaking parts of the world it is quite common. It seems that the Name itself carries no authority or power from God **unless the IDENTITY of the Son of God is invoked intentionally for God's purposes.** I am treading dangerous ground here but let us examine the evidence; it is just so important that we understand and use the Name of Jesus correctly:

a) The words **"Lord"** and **"Christ"** (Acts 2:36) are not names but titles surrounding the Name of **Jesus.**

b) The name of Jesus was fairly common in New Testament times, for example the robber **Barabbas** was himself known as **Jesus Barabbas,** according to some ancient manuscripts of Matt. 27:16-17. Likewise **Elymas** the sorcerer was also known as **Bar Jesus** (Acts 13:6) which means son of Jesus. Also in Paul's letter to the Colossians a Christian named Jesus had apparently been re named **Justus** (Col. 4:11). Jesus is a translation of the Hebrew name of **Joshua.**

c) The name Jesus has been bestowed upon many children in the poorer nations of the earth and in itself (dissociated from the **PERSON** of the Lord Jesus Christ) certainly carries no power to transform lives or lift people out of the curses of poverty and sickness.

d) The name of Jesus used in open or mindless blasphemy brings no blessing to the user, but rather the wrath of God. It brings the kind of response we can do without, sooner or later! (Exod. 20:7).

e)   It should not surprise us that many unclean spirits appropriate the name of Jesus for themselves, and as counterfeit spirits they answer to that name - Jesus.

7.3 EXPOSING FALSE JESUS SPIRITS

It is absolutely essential that ANY spirit being which appears to a human being must be questioned as to its identity and allegiance. You must not be afraid. You must question it (test the spirits - 1 John 4:1).

(a)   If it claims to be Jesus it should be asked if Jesus Christ came in the flesh (1 John 4:2-3), and flowing from that, if Jesus Christ:

(ii)   is the ONLY begotten Son of God (John 3:16)?

(iii)   ROSE again from the dead (Mark 16:6, 1 Cor. 15:12-20)?

(iv)   is now seated in Glory at the right Hand of our Almighty Father God (Heb. 1:3,13; 12:2)?

(v)   is now LORD of Lords and KING of Kings (Matt. 28:18, Rev. 17:14)? And

(vi)   is our Lord and our God (John 20:28)?

I think you will find that any spirit/angelic being that confronts you will either be able to answer positively ALL the above questions, OR be unable to affirm ANY of them. Likewise if the supposed *christophany* (appearance of Christ) cannot acknowledge these truths, it is obviously an enemy deception and not the REAL Jesus at all.

(b) If it claims to be an angel of God (e.g. Michael or Gabriel etc.) it must be asked the same questions and affirm the same truths as above. If it fails or refuses to do so, or gives you some smart, evasive "doubletalk" you know it is *a false angel of "light"* (2 Cor. 11:14).

Beware of the spirit of the False Prophet which one day will be cast into the Lake of Fire after it has deceived millions and caused much bloodshed (Rev. 16:13-14, 19:20, 20:10).

How important it is then, to be absolutely "focussed" or specific in calling on the One who is not only named *Jesus* but who is also *Lord* and *Christ* (Acts 2:36), and who is from Nazareth. My own favourite address to the unclean spirits which are to be cast out during a **Deliverance and Restoration meeting** has been **"In the Name of Jesus Christ of Nazareth ...**

Garth Cameron, a deliverance minister from Ballina, N.S.W. has an interesting testimony:

> *I was working with an Anglican Priest in counselling an alcoholic who was also a schizophrenic and we were commanding the demonic presence when a voice came from him saying, "Jesus says there are no more demons here". We commanded him to tell us his name. He said, "I am Jesus". We both recognised at the same time that we were dealing with a false Jesus. A. P. said, "You are lying".*

Voice: 'Are you calling me a liar'.

A.P. 'Not you R. (the person we were ministering to), we are speaking to the demon. I order you out in the name of Jesus Christ'.

We felt sure that it had left and R. was free.

> Remember always that there are many false Christs in the world today. Their work, appointed by Satan, is to lead, if possible, even the elect astray. *(Matt. 24:24).*

You can see from all this information that **counterfeit religious spirits** can be very destructive. The Lord Jesus Christ Himself told us that some will kill His disciples, thinking it as a service to God (John 15:18-16:4) and this, of course, has been proven true during the **Inquisition,** which lasted more than 200 years. So-called "heretics" were tortured and some 2000 burnt at the stake by one inquisitor alone **(T. Torquemada)** on behalf of the Pope.

Many Bible faith heroes were also burnt at the stake for their faith during the sixteenth century **Reformation,** not to mention the massacre of thousands of **Huguenots** (French Protestants) in August 1572.

The Lord Jesus Christ and Bible faith bring LIFE but religions and their controlling spirits minister DEATH, both SPIRITUALLY and PHYSICALLY!

7.4 SUMMARY

Most people will agree, after a little reflection, that human beings are ALL imbued with a religious nature. The tribes of the earth have been steeped historically in the worship of God or a god or gods in some form or other. Nature, the sun, the moon and various creatures or parts of creation have appeared to be vital to daily existence and therefore elevated to the rank of god(s). Ancestor worship is, of course, still widespread in many parts of the earth, and even those who deny the existence of a god/God, such as the humanists, unwittingly elevate THEMSELVES to the role of being gods, because they acknowledge no higher being to which they must give account of their lives in due time.

Yes, we human beings are all very religious, whether we acknowledge it or not. The Bible describes our bodies as a **house** (Gen. 4:7-8, Matt. 12:28-29, 43-45) which is really designed to become a **temple** of the Lord when the Holy Spirit is invited to make His dwelling within us (1 Cor. 3:16-17, 6:19-20). We need to remember the good Lord made us with three (3) parts or areas of life - **spirit, soul** and **body** (1 Thess. 5:23), so that we could become temples of God, not created by the hands of men (Acts 7:48-50) but by Him! Our bodies are to be the **outer courts** of His temples, the soul is designed to be the **Holy Place** which should be filled with His Holy Spirit, not a mess of unclean spirits squabbling for control. And, of course, the **born again human spirit** should reside in the **Holy of Holies** where we can unite with and be immersed in God's Spirit for REAL LIVING, serving the everlasting God in spirit and in truth (John 4:24).

From all of this it is easy to see that true religion can only be practised by those who have been born again (John 3:3-5) because, before the second (spiritual) birth takes place our human spirit is DEAD in trespasses and sins (Eph. 2:1). The second birth takes place when the Holy Spirit enters our bodies and gives life to our previously dead human spirit and together they set about making the human house a temple for God, and of God. This gives us great encouragement and comfort because it is only when the Holy Spirit indwells us that we KNOW we are children of God and really belong to Him (Rom. 8:9, 14-16).

However, until the Holy Spirit comes to dwell within us and take up His rightful position as Lord in our lives **we have a spiritual vacancy** which other spirits vie with each other to occupy and thereby control us as our Lord.

Hence the **Man of Sin** who *"takes his seat in the temple of God, proclaiming himself to be God"*. (2 Thess. 2:4-6).

When we see how much religiosity there is in the Church of God and add it to all the witchcraft and spiritism (talking to statues and the dead) etc., we begin to understand something of the mighty shaking and cleansing necessary before Christ can come for a Bride that is without spot or blemish. She may be considered without spot or blemish by legal covenant through the blood of Christ covering her sins, but experientially and in reality she is a long way from being ready for the Bridegroom. **It is a great mistake for Christians to settle for their legal position of being justified (forgiven) by faith, without also pursuing sanctification and Christlikeness. Clearly the Word of God encourages Christians to BE FOUND clean, as well as being RECKONED clean (2 Peter 3:13-14).** I am just so glad I am caught up in the Renewal movement of the Holy Spirit today and that the Lord is accelerating the necessary changes in my life.

> *Create in me a CLEAN heart O God, and renew a right spirit within me (Psalm 51:10)*

Please make sure you understand **the four points of definition** (section 4.5). I hope you find it very helpful in putting your own worship in Holy Spirit order, by the grace of the Lord.

Religiosity! You are rebuked and renounced in Jesus' mighty Name - loose me in Jesus Name!

By Oliphant for the Denver Post

"In a manner of speaking, what we lose on the merry-go-round we pick up on the swings!"

The tragedy is that the churches have not yet grasped the truth in this cartoon, that is, the HUGE NEED for the inner cleansing of the human soul from all its spiritual pollution.

APPENDIX "A"

ICONS and IMAGES

Definition of the Second Council of Nicaea, 787 A.D. Actio VII. Mansi, xiii. 378 D sqq.

*We define, with all care and exactitude, that the venerable and holy images are set up in just the same way as the figure of the precious and life-giving cross; painted images, and those in mosaic and those of other suitable material, in the holy churches of God, on holy vessels and vestments, on walls and in pictures, in houses and by the roadsides; images of our Lord and God and Saviour Jesus Christ and of our undefiled Lady, the holy God-bearer, and of the honourable angels, and of all saintly and holy men. For the more continually these are observed by means of such representations, so much the more will the beholders be aroused to recollect the originals and to long after them, and to pay to the images the tribute of an embrace and a reverence of honour, not to pay to them the actual worship which is according to our faith, and which is proper only to the divine nature: **For the honour paid to the image passes to its original, and he that adores an image adores in it the person depicted thereby ....***

THE WORD OF GOD

So much for the wisdom of men, which wisdom is often earthly, soulish and demonic (James 3:15). The Word of God says:

*"Take careful heed to yourselves, for **you saw no form** when the LORD spoke to you at Horeb out of the midst of the fire, **lest you act corruptly** and make for your-*

selves a carved image of the form of any figure: the like-
ness of male or female ...." (Deut. 4:15-16. cf v. 12).

Clearly the Lord explains why He keeps Himself INVIS-
IBLE. *It is to prevent us acting corruptly and making*
images. But does that stop the unclean religious spirit? Not
on your life! We make images anyway, even though we have
no idea what the originals looked like in the first place!

And to add insult to injury, we surround our images with
a pious, religious rationale to justify our rebellion. All the
cleverness of careful phrasing and explanations cannot hide
the fact that the Second Council of Nicaea, 787, greatly
erred in authorising the making and use of images for ANY
purpose, and thus misguided centuries of Christians to the
present day.

Don't forget contact with and talking to the dead (necro-
mancy) whether ancestors, family, friends or even Christians canonised as saints is an abomination to the Lord
(Deut. 18:9-14).

Our heavenly Father wants us to talk with HIM, in the Name
of His Son Jesus (John 14:6) OR talk with His Son Jesus
whom He has highly exalted (Phil. 2:9) and seated at His
right hand (Mark 16:19, Rom. 8:34 etc.)

The word *"anti"* means *"substitute"* in the New Testament
so when we reach out to other spirit beings instead of talking
to our heavenly Father or His Son we take an antichrist
position, and we show that we are not children of God who
are aware of having a heavenly Father (Matt. 6:9).

Let us receive this warning and, when the Church(es) experience the mighty SHAKING of God's Truth as this Age draws
to a close, let us heed the warning of the apostle John, *"Little*
children, keep yourselves from idols" (1 John 5:21).

APPENDIX "B"

DAILY SINNER'S PRAYER

It is vitally important that YOU believe that God is working out His plan to judge the earth and save for Himself as many as will repent and ask for mercy, and YOU REPENT and ASK FOR MERCY—the sooner the better. How about right now?

If you are not a Christian or if you are a Christian who has been slack and failed to follow the Lord Jesus the way you know you should, then you can put things straight with the Lord by saying a prayer along the following lines:

> Dear Lord Jesus,
>
> I am a sinner and I now know that I have done things which have grieved you. I am truly sorry Lord, for my sins.
>
> Please forgive me for ALL my sins. Wash me clean in your precious Blood. I renounce the devil, the powers of darkness and all their works in my life.
>
> I ask you, Lord Jesus, to break every foul curse upon my life, snap every unclean chain that binds me. Please FILL ME with your HOLY Spirit of power, and set me free to worship you and serve you as I should.
>
> Thank you, Lord Jesus, for making it all possible for me on Calvary's Cross, my Lord and my God.
>
> Hallelujah and Amen!

If you can agree with ALL these prayer points - that's great - get somewhere private and onto your knees and pray.

I suggest you don't READ this prayer out to the Lord but examine it and pray its PRINCIPLES out loud, from your HEART, using your own words if you can. If you read it, mean it.

If you can agree with some petitions but have difficulty with others you can at least make a beginning. As each day goes by your faith will increase and you should be able to pray more petitions. The Holy Spirit will help you - be persevering and patient.

This is a beginning, or a fresh start!

After this prayer has reconciled you to your Heavenly Father through the Lord Jesus Christ, you must move into contact with ALIVE Christians as soon as possible, preferably those who share the same kind of vision as in this book. There is not much point in joining a Church which belongs to the five foolish virgins group—they won't help you get clean and ready (Matt. 25:1-13). If you have any difficulty or even if everything goes smoothly for you, please 'phone us or write to us and tell us what you have done.

We know that God will provide a way forward for you to enter into the move of God's Spirit today and possess all that you want to possess. The only limitations are what you yourself impose, perhaps by failing to link with others who have caught fire.

We are here to help you if you need us.

MAY GOD BLESS YOU – in JESUS' Name!

Peter and Verlie Hobson

P.O. Box 1020
Crows Nest 1585
N.S.W., Australia

Tel:　61 2 9436 3657
Fax:　61 2 9437 6700
Email: judymt@tpg.com.au

APPENDIX "C"

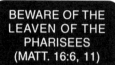

BEWARE OF THE LEAVEN OF THE PHARISEES (MATT. 16:6, 11)

PHARISEES
AND SCRIBES OF THE PHARISEES
RULERS (JOHN 11:57)
STRICT LAWKEEPING (MATT. 5:20)

FORM OF PIETY

Matt.	6:1-6	Before men
"	9:14	Fast often
"	23:1f	Condemned
Luke	7:36	Simon & sinner
"	18:10-14	With Tax-collector

TEACHING TRUTH

Deut.	17:10-11)	Moses
Matt.	23:1-6)	Seat
John	9:28-9)	
Acts	5:33-42	Gamaliel's wisdom
Acts	23:8	Resurrection, angel & spirit

HYPOCRITICAL

Matt.	6:1-6	Before men
"	6:16	Obvious fasting
"	7:1-5	Speck & Log
"	15:1-9	Traditions
Luke	13:10-17	Spirit of infirmity

NEAR THE TRUTH

Mark 12:28-34	Not far from the Kingdom of God

MONEY-LOVERS

Luke 16:14	God & mammon
Matt. 23:14	Devour widows' houses

MISGUIDED BELIEVERS

John	8:13,31, 44,59	
Acts	15:5	Circumcision of Moses

PROUD

Luke 18:10-14	With Tax-collector

TRUE BELIEVERS

John	3:1)	Nicodemus
"	7:50)	the ex-secret
"	19:39)	disciple
Acts	15:5	Circumcision Party
Acts	26:4-5)	
Phil.	3:5)	Apostle Paul

BEWARE OF THE LEAVEN OF THE PHARISEES (MATT. 16:6, 11)

TEACHING TRADITION
Matt. 15:1-9   Unwashed hands

PARTY LINE
John 7:47-48   Rulers believed?
Acts 23:6-8   "I am a Pharisee" appeal

DEFENSIVE
Matt. 19:3   Tested (divorce)
"   22:41-45   No more questions asked
Luke 5:30   Murmured (eat & drink)
"   6:7-8   Watched (Sabbath healing)
"   7:30   Rejected (re the Baptist)
John 11:47   What shall we do?
Luke 19:39-40 Silence your disciples

SCHEMERS
John 11:47) What shall we do?
Matt. 22:15) Took counsel
"   27:1) against Jesus
"   28:12)
Mark 3:6   )

TEACHING BLASPHEMY
Matt. 9:34) Beelzebul or
"   12:22-37) or the Spirit of God?

BLIND GUIDES
Matt. 15:14   Let them alone
"   23:16,17, Clean the
     19,26   inside, then the outside

VIPERS' OFFSPRING
Luke 3:7
Matt. 3:7
"   12:34
"   23:33

PUBLICATIONS BY THE SAME AUTHOR

This book is produced by FULL SALVATION FELLOWSHIP LTD., and designed to assist the people of God in their preparation for the drama of the End Time, which we believe has already begun on God's calendar.

The others published are:

> **"Guidance for Those Receiving Deliverance"**
> **"The Reincarnation Deception"** (out of print)
> **"Headcovering and Lady Pastor-Teachers"**
> **"Christian Authority and Power and the Stigmata"**
> **"Toronto and the Truths You Need to Know"**

Christian Deliverance series:

> Book 1 **"Make Yourselves Ready"**
> Book 2 **"Engaging the Enemy"**
> Book 3 **"Walking in Victory"**
> Book 4 **"We ALL Have Our Demons"**
> **"Your Full Salvation"**
> **"Surviving the Distress of Nations"**
> **"End-Time Deliverance and the Holy Spirit Revival"**
> **"Sex, Demons and Morality"**

Others in the process of production are:

> **"The Stigmata of Jesus"**
> **"Dissociate Identity Therapy-Help or Hoax?"**
> **"Sin is Demonic"**
> **"The Man of Sin"**

Ministry And Personal Enquiries

AUSTRALIA

Full Salvation Fellowship Ltd.
P.O. Box 1020
Crows Nest, 1585
AUSTRALIA

TEL: (02) 9436 3657
Fax: (02) 9437 6700
Website:wwwfullsalvationfellowship.com
Email: peter@fullsalvationfellowship.com

PHILIPPINES

Good News Kingsway Fellowship Int. Inc.
P.O. Box 6
CAGAYAN DE ORO CITY 9000
PHILIPPINES

Phone: 088 857 3485

Full Salvation Fellowship
Hillside, Purok 4-A Gusa
9000 Cagayan de Oro City
PHILIPPINES

Email : fidel@eudoramail.com

UNITED KINGDOM

Ellel Ministries
Ellel Grange
Ellel, Lancaster, LA2 OHN
U.K.

Phone: (0) 1524 751651
Fax: (0) 1524 751738
Email : info@grange.ellel.org.uk

U.S.A.

Impact Christian Books, Inc.
332 Leffingwell Ave., Suite 101
Kirkwood
Mo 63122 USA

Phone: (314) 822 3309
Fax: (314) 822 3325

AFRICA

SJBS Outreach Inc.
P.O. Box 4953 Oshodi
Lagos, NIGERIA
WEST AFRICA

Adekeye World Outreach
P.O. Box 1413, OSOGBO
Osun State, NIGERIA
WEST AFRICA

Phone: 035 241 423

Evang. Frank Williams Aboagye
P.O. Box SE2254
KUMASI – SUAME
GHANA, W. AFRICA

Full Salvation Ministry
P.O. Box 3438, KISII
KENYA, EAST AFRICA

Fax to Box (254) 381 31194
Email : benwelasiago@hotmail.com

Full Salvation Ministry of Uganda
Ps. Grace Okurut
P.O. Box 25643
KAMPALA
UGANDA, EAST AFRICA

Phone: (077) 453 745
Email: okurutg@yahoo.com

Trade Enquiries

AUSTRALIA

W.A. Buchanan and Co.,
P.O. Box 469
KIPPA RING, QLD, 4021

Phone: (07) 3883 4022
Fax: (07) 3883 4033
Email: service@wab.com.au

NEW ZEALAND

Rise Up Marketing NZ
P.O. Box 345
Warkworth, New Zealand

Phone: 0800 747 387
Fax: (09) 425 6727
Email: info@riseup.co.nz

PHILIPPINES

Full Salvation Fellowship
Hillside, Purok 4 – A Gusa
9000 Cagayan de Oro City
PHILIPPINES

Email: fidel@eudoramail.com

UNITED KINGDOM

Ellel Ministries
Ellel Grange
Ellel, Lancaster, LA2 OHN
ENGLAND

Phone: (0) 1524 751651
Fax: (0) 1524 751738
Email: info@grange.ellel.org.uk

U.S.A.

Impact Christian Books, Inc.
332 Leffingwell Ave., Suite 101
Kirkwood
Mo 63122 USA

Phone: (314) 822 3309
Fax: (314) 822 3325

AFRICA

SJBS Outreach Inc.
P.O. Box 4953 Oshodi
Lagos, NIGERIA
WEST AFRICA

Frank Williams Aboagye
P.O. Box SE 2254
KUMASI – SUAME
GHANA, W. AFRICA

Full Salvation Ministry
P.O. Box 3438 KISII
KENYA, EAST AFRICA
Email: benwelasiago@hotmail.com
        fsm@pace-tech.co.ke

Full Salvation Ministry of Uganda
Ps. Grace Okurut
P.O. Box 25643
KAMPALA
UGANDA, EAST AFRICA

Phone: (077) 453 745
Email: okurutg@yahoo.com

Comments on our Publications

"I rejoice and give special thanks to Him for the first two of your books... You don't know how encouraging it was for us to read your books..."
> Peter Horrobin, Director of Ellel Ministries
> Lancaster, England

"I have been blessed by EVERY book you have written ... I have read many books on Warfare and Deliverance, from Derek Prince, Don Basham, Neil Anderson, Unger, Hobart Freeman, etc., but your books spell it out just as it is, in LOVE and TRUTH. I pray every Pastor and every man and woman of God reads these books..."
> Lorraine Clifford
> Bundaberg, QLD. Australia

"Great stuff ..."
> G. Milton Smith
> New Zealand, Principal of Faith Bible Course and
> Author of the classic, "God Acting in History" and others

"Your teaching reminds me of that of Derek Prince, whom I respect very much."
> Pastor Paul O'Sullivan
> Northern Beaches Christian Centre, Sydney.

"...*provide(s) fresh insight* into some areas of the deliverance ministry that I have not seen in print in this country."
> Don Rogers, Director
> Spiritual Warfare Ministries
> Warrington, Penn., U.S.A.

"The Books (Book 1 and Book 2) are *excellent textbook material* on the Deliverance Ministry ... they have been a blessing to me, and I might add eye-opening and heart

challenging, especially for these End Times ... *"Make Yourselves Ready" is a classic on casting out demons ... practical* ... would be immense help ..."
Pastor Kevin Wedrat, A.O.G.
Goondiwindi, Australia

"Thank God I picked up your books ..."
Pastor M. Olive
Sheffield, England

"I have just read with great interest and increasing excitement your books which speak to us powerfully."
Doug Smart
London, England

"I have been greatly blessed by Brother Peter Hobson's books ... and will be most grateful for ... a complete list."
Ps Richard Smith
New Jersey, U.S.A.

"I have found your books exciting, educational, Scripture based and affirming and strengthening for what we have already been involved in."
D. Salyers
Wentzville, U.S.A.

"I find Peter Hobson's material tremendously encouraging and challenging ... How I praise the Lord for your ministry in these End-Times."
Brian Newton
E. Yorkshire, England

"I sincerely wish to commend you, your ministry and the various booklets you have produced over the years as they are vital parts of the ministry of our Lord shared with us while He was with us on earth ... for diligently continuing to

bring this vital area of ministry to Christian peoples awareness."
Raymond Day
The Bible Society in AUSTRALIA

"I have been blessed with your publications and encourage you to continue to do all that you can to open the eyes of the sleeping Church and urge them to get set free, committed and obedient to the Word of God or in time they will fall away ... your words are true ... (do) not stop at any cost!"
David Kriss (Jewish prophet)
Nth Balwyn, Vic., Australia

"... Peter Hobson's series are written very simply but carry authority, experience and balance, giving scriptural answers and equipment against problems caused by satanic influences and works..."
"Pastor's Study" Jan 1988
A.O.G. in AUSTRALIA

"I have read books on deliverance and put them aside. *Yours carry the power and love of God,* a protected by the Holy Spirit feeling."
Sheilah Dahanayaka
Nugegoda, Sri Lanka

"Now I am in India and experience the greatest anointing, success in ministering Christ's power I ever have. Amazing deliverances are taking place here. A friend in Madras lent me a copy of your book, *"Christian Deliverance" Book 2.* That was my first knowledge of your ministry, and I *became blessed with your insight and experience and soundness."*
Norwegian Missionary
Kristian Sand, Nilgiris, South India

MAJOR NEW BOOK!

SYNOPSIS

"WE ALL HAVE OUR DEMONS"

This book basically reveals that what Hollywood has been presenting for 20 years is actually Bible truth. It is a result of 30 years experience as Christian exorcists (deliverance ministers).

The heart disease of original sin is SPIRITUAL. It is so simple, so obvious and the churches have been so blind! Indeed it may scorch the paint (or cement) off the church walls.

The book explains how easy it is to increase our level of sin disease (demonisation) by our behaviour patterns, and looks at the most common forms we humans suffer (fear, stupidity, rebellion, life-threatening infirmity, stress, mental illness, superstition, etc.).

Special chapters deal with cancer, death, religious spirits and mind problems such as multiple personality, dissociate identity, and false memory syndrome.

Deceptions such as reincarnation and superstition are explained as well as the mystery of the biblical Man of Sin revealed. This is necessary before the return of Christ (2 Thess. 2:2-4).

It is not a book of condemnation, it is a book which offers hope to those who suffer without relief. It makes change possible where it once seemed impossible.

We have tried to present spiritual truths in a way most people can understand but, because scholars need hard evidence, some sections in the second half are tailored for serious Bible students.

We hope it makes a difference.

Peter and Verlie Hobson.